Family Matters

The Role of Christianity in the Formation of the Western Family

Family Matters

The Role of Christianity in the Formation of the Western Family

by Anthony J. Guerra

PARAGON HOUSE

St. Paul, Minnesota

First Edition, 2002

Published in the United States by
Paragon House
2700 University Avenue West
St. Paul, MN 55114

Library of Congress Cataloging-in-Publication Data

Guerra, Anthony J.
    Family matters : the role of Christianity in the formation of the western family / by Anthony J. Guerra.
        p. cm.
    Includes bibliographical references and index.
    ISBN 1-55778-810-3 (alk. paper)
        1. Family--Religious aspects--Christianity--History of doctrines. I. Title.

BT707.7 G84 2002
261.8'3585'09—dc21

                                                          2001051009

10 9 8 7 6 5 4 3 2 1

For current information about all releases from Paragon House,
visit the web site at http://www.paragonhouse.com

This book is dedicated to the memory of
Young Jin nim
who lived and continues to live
for the sake of true love

Acknowledgments

When first conceiving of this book project a few days before Christmas 1994, I was predisposed to think that Christianity's impact on the family was at best limited and somewhat mixed. I thought, for instance, that certainly the elevated status of celibacy in some quarters of Christianity was an unequivocal negative for the family in the West. Almost all of my initial presuppositions have been substantially revised and several have been virtually inverted in the course of my work on this book. During much of my research and writing of this book, I was employed as a full-time University administrator working typically a sixty-hour week. I am grateful for the opportunity to return to Harvard Divinity School as a visiting scholar in the academic year 2000-2001 where I was able to complete the writing of the manuscript. Some nearly twenty years ago at Harvard, I labored as a doctoral student on articles on Tertullian and Justin Martyr as well as a book on Paul—celibate men or men struggling to be celibate as I was then.

The individuals who have encouraged and enlightened me in the course of my work are legion. I will mention only a few of them here. I am especially grateful to Farley and Betsy Jones, good friends, who read the material and gave invaluable feedback. Professors Thomas Selover and Wilson Kimnach generously offered their insights and comments at several stages of the work. I am very thankful to Debby Sands who remained committed to the task of typing the manuscript and the more arduous one of deciphering my handwriting even after she had moved from New England to Texas. I am grateful to the staff of Paragon House. I must mention by name Rosemary Byrne Yokoi and Gordon Anderson whose editorial comments have been edifying. Most of all, I am grateful to my good wife and seven children as they have waited long for me to fully realize Family Matters.

Cambridge, MA
March, 2002

CONTENTS

Introduction

THE THESIS

The present work documents the influence of religion, specifically Christianity, on the development of family life in the West. While it is certainly true that other factors impact the life of the family, the thesis argued here is that none has been more significant than religion and no surrogate has yet been found for its beneficial influence on the family. To state my conclusion in advance, the healthy family as we know it today would not exist but for the profound influence of religion, especially Christianity, through the ages.

Political and economic factors do represent significant limiting factors in familial relationships, whether they be between husband and wife or parent and child. Dire economic conditions may necessitate the abandonment of one or more children in order to assure the survival of other family members—a tragic dilemma which parents faced throughout most of Western history and which still pertains to several stricken lands. Yet the manner of the abandonment and the consequent life of the abandoned, as well as the affective relationships among the remaining family members, will be determined more by their cultural and attitudinal perspectives, than by economic factors.

Likewise, political factors can restrict familial expression, including size of the family, but the quality of family life will be most significantly determined by cultural and particularly religious factors. Social psychologists have noted that associational patterns and the nature of commitment in religious and familial institutions have much in common, and differ importantly from those of political, economic and educational institutions.[1] This may be one of the reasons that governments have been so unsuccessful in remedying family problems.

For much of the twentieth century, the American government has expanded its sovereignty and services, thus displacing private philanthropy and especially religious charitable efforts. For a time, government appeared to be omnipotent and capable of solving all human problems as long as the renderings unto Caesar were progressively enhanced. In upholding the sacrosanct cause of separating church and state, the federal government refused to fund social programs, however effective, that were faith-based. In effect the state contributed to a view of religion as entirely privatized, having at best minimal public significance or relevance. Paradoxically, in the last quarter of the twentieth century, the state has been widely criticized for its ineptitude in dealing with social ills, in particular the problem-plagued American family.

THE PROBLEM: THE CONTEMPORARY FAMILY

Certainly the traditional family in the United States is presently endangered. Yet, even in the most at-risk group, inner city minority families, some succeed in overcoming the destructive forces arrayed against them. Along with middle-class families as well as the wealthiest Americans,[2] these families claim that religion is a key factor in their success, endurance and happiness. As skepticism concerning the usefulness of state interventions in family matters grows, we would do well to pay closer attention to the power of religion to sustain and fortify families.

I should state at the outset that no one religion has a monopoly on this power; further, religions with strongly differing theologies, both liberal and conservative, have measurable positive influence on families. Furthermore, although in this work I will be focusing on Christianity, the available evidence suggests that synagogues, temples and mosques are equally efficacious agents for fostering strong families. The great divide seems to be between those who participate in religious practice and those without religious involvement.

Let us review briefly some of the secular cultural forces currently impacting the American family. The American entertainment industry, particularly popular films, represent as well as shape prevailing societal attitudes and trends. In this regard, popular films targeted at children and general audiences may be the most revealing.

Contemporary American films have popularized the myth that children almost always have better judgment than their parents concerning critical life decisions. Walt Disney has virtually displaced the motif "Father knows best" with that of "Father as quintessentially clueless." In the wildly successful animated film, *The Little Mermaid*, the father needs to be enlightened by his more savvy and tolerant daughter, Ariel, before conflict resolution can occur. The proposed marriage of Ariel is stereotypically represented as an act of defiance toward the father and his values. A happy ending is reached when the father realizes the error of his ways and blesses the union. In *Aladdin*, Jasmine's royal father is even more pathetic, unwittingly controlled by his evil vizier and his parrot. In this case, the father will be saved by his daughter's unlikely suitor, who would otherwise be totally unacceptable to him as a future son-in-law. Without explanation, throughout both *The Little Mermaid* and *Aladdin*, a mother is totally absent. Perhaps it would have been distasteful for the Disney producers to represent an equally inept mother. However, to present a competent and wise maternal figure would contradict the prevailing ideology of "children know best," thus leaving as the only alternative the omitting of the role of mother altogether. While popular culture may frown upon negative characterizations of mothers, it is not ready to accept a "Mother knows much" model, effectively diminishing its ideal of the self-sufficient, streetwise youth.

The tradition of parents playing a constructive role in the courtship process of their daughters is rarely, if ever, countenanced in contemporary films. Obviously, such films prefer daring romantic exploits of adolescents who are portrayed as knowing better than their benighted parents.

To be sure, *Aladdin* and *The Little Mermaid* are among the least objectionable popular entertainment offerings targeting family audiences, including their youngest members. Many of us could rejoice if the model of "Father knows best" were replaced by that of the greater collective wisdom of a father and mother guiding their children. Such a model, however, is not being offered.

More troubling than the productions of Hollywood, however, is the reality of increasing numbers of American children living in one-parent families. There is also the growing prevalence of no-parent families, wherein a teenage mother, who is likely to have herself been raised by an unwed mother, presides.

In 1981, Sar Levitan and Richard Belous wrote that "the predominance of the traditional household (a husband, wife, and children) is being challenged."[3] By 1995, only 36 percent of American families could be classified as traditional.[4] The 2000 census shows that only 23.5 percent of American households are made up of married couples with their children.[5] The percentage of family groups with children under eighteen years old headed by one parent has grown from 13 percent in 1970 to 31

percent in 1994.[6] Only 51 percent of children lived in a household with their two parents in 1998 and 18.2 percent of children were living with single parents.[7] Further, a staggering 65
percent of all black families with children under eighteen years
old are led by one parent.[8] Meanwhile, the percentage of white
one-parent families with children under eighteen years old has
more than doubled since 1970.[9] As Elaine May notes, "Gradually and ironically the 'normative' American family is coming to
resemble family patterns that have historically been typical of
'marginalized' Americans."[10] The trend of white teenagers bear-
ing their children out of wedlock evidences this pattern. Presently, half of all births in New York City are illegitimate.[11] Sena-
tor Patrick Moynihan has said about the rise in illegitimacy in
the United States: "No society has ever dealt with this kind of
thing. It has hit us like a cyclone…"[12] According to Sara S.
McLanahan, "Children who grow up with only one of their biological parents (nearly always the mother) are disadvantaged across
a broad array of outcomes. They are twice as likely to drop out
of high school, 2.5 times as likely to become teen mothers, and
1.4 times as likely to be idle—out of school and out of work—as
children who grow up with both parents."[13]

For some time, juvenile delinquency, particularly violent
crime, has been rising even while the overall crime rate has been
declining. According to Peter Greenwood, "Between 1984 and
1992, the number of juveniles arrested for homicide, who were
under the age of fifteen, increased by 50 percent."[14] In ten states
studied, the juvenile violent offenses cases increased by 18 percent from 1985 through 1989.[15] Between 30 and 40 percent of
all boys growing up in urban areas in America will be arrested
before their eighteenth birthday.[16] In 1950, the Gluecks published their work reporting that they were able to predict juve-

nile delinquency from an early age based on family background. Although for some decades criminologists resisted the explanation that broken homes had an effect on crime, the experts have provided overwhelming evidence. In the words of Travis Hirschi, "An immense amount of research later, we know better. At the neighborhood or community level, rates of family disruption (measured by the percentage of single-headed families or the divorce rate) are major predictors of the crime rate."[17] Robert J. Sampson, Professor of Sociology at the University of Chicago and research fellow at the American Bar Foundation, has noted that single-parent homes, not race, is the determining factor in the rates of violent crimes: "...family structure, especially percentage [of] single-parent families, helps account for the association between race and violent crime: racial composition was not significantly related to rates of violent crime when percentage [of] single-parent families were controlled."[18]

The total percentage of U.S. children living with both parents has declined steadily from 1970, when it was 85 percent, to 1994, when only 69 percent lived with both parents.[19] This decline is attributable not only to out-of-wedlock births, but also to the increasing incidence of divorce. Since 1975, at least one million children per year have experienced the divorce of their parents.[20]

Apart from the issue of the higher crime rate of children from single-parent families is the psychic suffering many children of divorced parents endure. Sar Levitan and Richard Belous noted in 1981 the significantly diminished social pressures to keep a marriage going even if children are involved. While the vast majority of American adults believe that a child raised by one parent in a broken home will face many added difficulties, five out of seven of these same adults still believe it is socially permissible for a married couple to get a divorce when they cannot get along, even if they have children.[21] Judith S. Wallerstein, who conducted the longest study tracking divorced families ever attempted, writes that in 1971, when she began her study, she viewed divorce and its effects as a "brief crisis that would resolve itself. By the end of the decade, however, several researchers including myself had begun to recognize that divorce is a much more serious trauma."[22] When Wallerstein and her researchers conducted follow-up interviews one year to eighteen months later, they found "most families still in crisis. Their wounds were wide open…"[23] Five years later, their reviews resulted in the researchers being "deeply concerned about a large number of youngsters—well over a third of the whole group—who were significantly worse off than before. Clinically depressed…early disturbances, such as sleep problems, poor learning or acting out, had become chronic."[24] Wallerstein found very worrisome the difference between the 1970 and 1980 reports from mental health clinics: "…many more troubled, even suicidal children. I am very worried about the acute depression in many adolescents who functioned well before the divorce."[25] Further, as Sara S. McLanahan has observed, remarriage is not a quick fix for these children as "children of stepfamilies don't do better than children of mothers who never remarry."[26]

In 1986, after parking my car on Main Street in the downtown area of a small upper middle-class town, I encountered a little girl, perhaps ten years old, sobbing uncontrollably as her mother admonished her not to dare "ruin this relationship for me" while the mother's male companion stood by listlessly. The mother added that her daughter should forget the dream that she would return to her father. The problem, which I will return to later, is that despite the efforts of the film industry and the words of the apparently recently divorced mother, children can't forget!

Can government adequately address this problem? As will be discussed below, probably not. In a recent study, Donald Critchlow concluded that despite enormous costs in the 1970s and 1980s, federal family planning failed to reduce the number of out-of-wedlock births.[27] Fortunately, some correcting trends have emerged in the 1990s and seem to be persisting. For instance, after having risen to its highest point ever in 1988, the percentage of unmarried black women giving birth did begin to decline, and by 1996 had reached its lowest level in 40 years.[28] After 1994, the birthrate among unwed white women also began to drop.[29] Given the fact that sexually active teenagers in 1995 got pregnant at a higher rate than they did in 1988, it would seem that abstention must have been a key factor.[30] It appears that the initiation of teenage abstinence campaigns in the late 1980s throughout America by Christian leaders, as described later in this work, is having an impact.

A Limited Option: Government and the Family

In recent years, several social commentators have questioned whether it is possible that any governmental policy and programs can be strengthening to families. At least three widely representative positions on the issue of the potential effectiveness of governmental family policy are current in the United States.

The first, and perhaps most representative viewpoint of the proper role of government with respect to families and family policymaking is the instrumentalist perspective. Partial to such a view, President Clinton in the first Presidential debate of October, 1996 referred to government as a "tool" to help people. There can be no moral imperative for government to support any particular kind of family, traditional or otherwise; rather, government should aid all groupings of people in need who define themselves as family.[31] It is the state's responsibility to guarantee a minimal living standard to all its people as it responds to the consequences of personal tragedy, family dysfunction and social disintegration. As Levitan and Belous see it, "the expansion of the welfare state has been more a reaction to the [these] developments than their cause."[32]

Contrary to the instrumentalist, the traditionalist believes the welfare state to be inherently inimical to the family. One of its most articulate spokespersons, Allan Carlson, blames the modern welfare state for the progressive displacement of the family:

> "While the industrial corporations took control over most production tasks, the welfare state seized or absorbed an array of what had been for thousands of years, family functions regarding 'dependency': the care and security of the aged, the shelter and care of the handicapped and the sick, the practical moral, sexual and cultural education of children and youth, the provision of medical care, the care of infants and small children and protection after accident or crisis."[33]

From the vantage point of the traditionalist, most of the historical functions of the family have been assumed by the corporate state. This is the primary cause of the modern family's weakness and decline. The welfare state as a universal caregiver weakens the incentive to enter and maintain a marriage relationship which rests on the promise of mutual care "...in sickness or in health, ...until death do us part." According to Carlson, only in a welfare state society can high levels of divorce, cohabitation and illegitimacy occur as the government "...offers itself as a lifetime 'spouse' ever ready to care for one's sores, listen to one's complaints, and take responsibility for one's children. Quite simply, 'husbands' and 'wives'—as social categories—are no longer needed."[34] A central item of the traditionalists' critique of the modern state is that it subsidizes the irresponsible behavior of out-of-wedlock births at the expense of intact families, upon which it imposes heavier taxes. The tax burden in turn discourages the creation or maintenance of such families. The logical conclusion of the traditionalist analysis is that government welfare programs should be drastically curtailed or abolished. Only this will remedy our contemporary malady.

A third position is represented by the pragmatists, who shy away from either theoretical or moralistic assessments of government family policies and rather focus on their outcomes. Pragmatists, however, note that the inveterate American predisposition against government intervention in private matters, most especially family affairs, is a powerful constraint on successful state family policy making, especially in an age when many Americans feel their society is over-regulated and over-organized. Further, in *The Futility of Family Policy*, Gilbert Steiner refers to a more formidable practical objection to family policy making, namely "…the diversity of family forms and styles is simply too great to be encompassed by a national policy, that what is dysfunction in one family may be quite tolerable in another."[35] From the pragmatists' perspective, the politics of family policy is unworkable; effective organization for family policy is not feasible because as soon as one leaves the general theme and confronts the details of family regulation, the consensus collapses and "family policy splits into innumerable components. Its many causes with many votaries."[36] Thus, family policy is more like the themes of peace, justice and freedom: in the abstract there are no dissenters, but practical legislative proposals for their realization are highly divisive. Accordingly, pro-family legislation is no contest for, say, medical care for the aged, where the elderly constituency will provide a fairly unanimous base of support against the highly splintered advocacy groups so typical for any child or family bill. The foundational insight of the pragmatists' view is that the state is inherently incapable of affecting the "stuff" of strong families: "Government has no mechanism to enforce love, affection, and concern between husband and wife, between parent and child, or between one sibling and another."[37]

If the role of the state is at best an effectively limited one, then to whom can families in crisis turn today?

AN ENDURING HOPE: THE SOCIAL SCIENCES ON RELIGION AND THE FAMILY

In the August 1996 cover story of *The Atlantic Monthly*, "Welcome to the Next Church," concerning the growth of megachurches around the United States, Charles Trueheart quotes a returned church-goer, Bonnie Leetma: "Our government has let us down. Our workplace is not secure. Our communities are falling apart. Churches and synagogues are serving the community. It's been the best kept secret of the last couple of decades."[38] There is, in fact, a growing body of social scientific evidence to corroborate Ms. Leetma's assertion of a positive and decisive role of religion in solving some of America's most intractable social problems. Joseph Califano, an architect of Lyndon Johnson's Great Society and currently director of Columbia University's Center on Addiction and Substance Abuse, has said that he was surprised when, on a tour of Center programs, nearly every ex-drug addict he met cited religious belief as a key to rehabilitation.[39] According to Harvard economist Richard Freeman, boys who regularly attend church are 50 percent less likely to engage in crime than boys of similar backgrounds who do not attend church; they are 54 percent less likely to use drugs and 47 percent less likely to drop out of school.[40] Another concern already mentioned, the rate of teenage suicide, is significantly affected by both family and religious connections. Steven Stacks found that as the importance of the domestic and religious affiliations declined, the rate of suicide both for the general population and especially for the "young cohort" rose.[41] Given the vital relationship between societal well-being and the strength of families, a central question that must be addressed is, "What impact does religion have on families?"

Up until the late 1970s, there was a dearth of social scientific research and publications on the connection between family and religion.[42] Beginning with academic psychology in the 1920s and 30s, interest in religion was perceived as evidence of unscientific orientation. As early as 1921, it was shown that scientists, especially psychologists, were less religious than most of the American population.[43] Scientists in the 1930s may have felt that science had won the long war with religion and there was little to be learned from it. Moreover, the legacy from the work of Freud and early social scientists promoted the expectation that only social misfits were likely to be involved with and rely on religious institutions. Beginning with Rodney Stark's 1971 review of this hypothesis, a number of rigorous scientific studies have debunked the assertion of a negative relationship between religiosity and social competency.[44] Indeed, since the late 1970s, a substantive body of social scientific literature has demonstrated the positive relationship between religion and healthy families.

While the United States has the highest divorce rate among

Western nations, there are several areas of the United States where the divorce rate is significantly lower. The proportion of Americans who are divorced tends to be low in areas where church membership is high, "such as the Upper Plains states, Utah, the Hispanic areas of Texas and parts of the Southeast."[45] Conversely, the proportion of divorced people is higher in such areas as the West Coast and in Ohio, Illinois, Michigan, and Florida which have low church membership.[46] Likewise, the areas where church membership is high have a higher proportion of two-parent families with children.[47]

Although industrialization and the corresponding change from a household production economy to a family-wage economy (often proposed as the central explanation for the rise in the U.S. divorce rate) has been progressing for two centuries in America, the family in 1950 was impressively stable. In 1960, 69 percent of Americans were affiliated with particular churches. After 1960, the number appreciably decreased; correspondingly the national divorce rate began to rise dramatically.[48] During the 1960s and 1970s, while the importance and centrality of religion to Americans declined, as did their confidence in religious institutions and authorities, two related phenomena appeared: the marriage rate fell dramatically and cohabitation emerged as a significant alternative lifestyle.[49]

It should be noted that in virtually all instances social scientists studying the relationship between religion and social, especially familial well-being, are concerned not with the nominal religious identity of individuals, but rather with the attitudinal and particularly behavioral characteristics marking their religious involvement. Most commonly, the researchers' standards of measurement are straightforwardly objective, such as the frequency of participation in religious services or individual prayer. Al-

though religious identity through birth alone may be less defining than other natal attributes, social scientists indicate that the
religious attitudes and behavior of parents do influence their
children's religious as well as social thinking and behavior.

In 1992, three sociologists published in the *American Journal of Sociology* the results of their investigation of the extent to
which eighteen year olds' cohabitational and marital experiences
are related to their mother's as well as their own religious commitments and involvements.[50] Using mainstream Protestants as
a control group, the researchers found that both males and females without religious affiliations have cohabitational rates that
are approximately 50 percent higher than those for the control
group.[51] The researchers documented that people without religious affiliation opt less for marriage than those with religious
affiliation.[52] Further, the researchers found that the mother's religiosity also influenced the cohabitative and marital behavior of
young people.[53] In a separate study, sociologists found a strong
correlation between adolescent attitudes and sexual behavior and
religious involvement. They concluded that "young people who
attend church frequently and who have religion in their lives
have the least permissive attitudes and are less experienced sexually."[54] The Jensens' findings in *Psychology Reports* recorded not
only that religious people have stronger family values, but also
specifically that increased religiosity in men is reflected in their
becoming more similar to women in family values.[55] I shall return later to the issue of the importance of religion for the domestication of males in Western history.

Despite the problems in American families, some, including
Afro-American families living in the inner cities, are doing well.
What is the decisive factor in these families' success? Both the
quantitative as well as qualitative social scientific evidence points

to religion as a decisive factor in strengthening these families.

There is no city in the United States for which there is more systematic data for comparison over the last 50 years than Middletown, U.S.A.[56] Discussing the association between religiosity and several types of family behavior, two sociologists, Howard M. Bahr and Bruce A. Chadwick, compared indicators of family life and religious practices in Middletown in 1925 and 1977-78.[57] Bahr and Chadwick note that, in terms of marital satisfaction and stability, there was no significant difference between Catholics and Protestants but there appears appreciable differences between persons who report a church preference and those with no preference. They observe that "the latter are over represented among the single/never married, the remarried, and the divorced/separated, and are correspondingly underrepresented in the married (first marriage) category."[58] Church attendance is also significantly correlated to marital happiness; at the upper extreme of "very satisfied" a full 60 percent of the more frequent attenders perceive their marriages as very satisfactory, compared with 43 percent of others.[59] The authors conclude that the more religious residents of Middletown were more likely to be married, to remain married, and to be highly satisfied with their marriages.[60] Upon comparing the Middletown data with the National Opinion Research Center (NORC) at the University of Chicago Public Use Surveys for 1977-78, they also concluded that the positive relationship between religion and family in Middletown pertains as well to the rest of the country: "In the United States as a whole, church-goers are more likely to be married, less likely to be divorced or single, more likely to manifest high levels of marital satisfaction, and less likely to have very small families.[61]

The evidence that religion is positively related to marital stability is quite strong. This body of literature, of course, lends credence to the hypothesis that religion is a primary force reducing marital dissolution. This is not an insignificant accomplishment, to be sure, in an age when the term "culture of divorce" (indicating the societal preference for divorce, rather than other solutions, for troubled couples) has been coined.

There is even stronger social science evidence confirming a positive relationship between religiosity and marital adjustment or happiness, suggesting a more expansive role for religion than that of reducing divorce rates. Kip Jenkins, in his important review article of the sixty years of social scientific literature (1930 -1990), gives his highest rating of "strong" to the evidence supporting the thesis that "high religiosity in home promotes family happiness and success."[62]

Erik Filsinger and Margaret Wilson collected data through an extensive questionnaire of 208 married couples from churches in a large metropolitan area. The sample was stratified by religious denomination to arrive at a cross section of fundamental and liberal Protestant churches.[63] Although sociologists have long considered the socio-economic status of couples as critical to marital happiness, the results indicated that "...religiosity explained roughly twice as much variance as did socio-economic rewards or family development characteristics."[64] Simply put, the greater the religiosity, the higher the marital adjustment: "Religiosity was the most consistent and strongest predictor of marital adjustment."[65] Melvin L. Wilkinson and William C. Tanner, in their study of Mormon adolescents, found that the measure of religious commitment as determined by church attendance was "the key causal variable" in their perceptions of family affection.[66] Religiosity was shown to have far greater significance in determining family happiness than such factors as social class, age and length of marriage, and even the measure of family activities.[67] In an earlier study of 453 college students, researcher M. A. Johnson found that religious students tended to perceive their families as happier, warmer and more accepting than non-religious students.[68]

One surprising area where religion makes a difference for married couples is in the level of sexual satisfaction. In *The Social Organization of Sexuality*, sociologists from the University of Chicago and the State University of New York at Stony Brook describe their own findings as "counterintuitive", namely that religious women achieve greater satisfaction in sexual intercourse with their husbands than do non-religious women.[69] The authors report that "...women without religious affiliation were the least likely to report always having an orgasm with their primary partner...In general, having a religious affiliation was associated with higher rates of orgasm for women...the discrepancies, however, between the two groups are of sufficient magnitude to suggest that religion may be independently associated with rates of female orgasm."[70] As we shall see, from an historical perspective these findings are far less surprising than contemporary views might presume.[71]

A weighty and growing body of social science literature finds that people who are involved religiously not only tend to engage less frequently in pre-marital sex, but also are prone to marry in higher percentages and to remain married longer. Further, the more religious tend to enjoy happier marriages, including more satisfying sexual relationships between the marital partners, than do the less religious. It seems that the integration of sexuality within healthy interpersonal relationships is assisted by a couple's shared religious commitment. The cliché that "the family that prays together, stays together" is plainly borne out by a preponderance of the social scientific literature.

In the main, the approach of this study is historical, examining the pivotal moments when Christianity succeeded in transforming the often brutal norms and practices defining the Western family. The intent here is not to provide an exhaustive review of the relationship between church and family but rather to provide access for the reader to those central moments of Christianity's efforts to reform the family in accord with its founder's insights: the divine origin of the institution of marriage; the marital union as a life-long commitment between equals and the affirmation that all children are special and worthy of respect and loving care.

The transcendent referent of religion seems to allow the believer greater confidence and openness to transform, reform and renew the Western family. If the family is the cornerstone of society, Christianity's battle for the family, as described in the following pages, is in fact a battle for the health, peacefulness and prosperity of Western society.

1

The Thousand-Year Campaign: The Church Battles to Reform Marriage

Much of the contemporary debate on the family takes for granted that the cluster of family values commonly referred to as "traditional", including marriage as a life-long monogamous commitment, mutual fidelity of husband and wife, and parental willingness to make sacrifices for the welfare and proper rearing of children, are the ready heritage of Western civilization. The long and bitter struggle to reverse the brutal ancient and medieval family norms wherein coercive sex and child abandonment were both legitimate and widely practiced by the power elite is forgotten or, perhaps more accurately, unknown. An historical recounting of the valiant and determined efforts of ecclesiastical leaders to promote an alternative, more humanitarian model of marriage and family illustrates the thesis advanced in the Introduction that religion is a vital force in the formation and maintenance of healthy family life, and indeed has been such a force for nearly two millennia.

In the popular consensus, it is imagined that the attraction to Christianity of Constantine the Great in 312 C.E. represents the beginning of a soon fully realized transformation of the social order of the Roman Empire, which transformation endures throughout the Middle Ages, only to be disrupted by the revolutionary periods of the Enlightenment and modernity. In fact, however, Christian family values and practices in its early and formative periods were as much influenced by its social contexts—Hebraic and Hellenistic—as it influenced them. Centuries were needed before the distinctive emphasis of the marital values reflected in the teachings of Jesus had measurable impact on European society. Second- and third-century Christian literature staked out Christianity's position against the popular culture while relying heavily upon marriage ideals advocated by the counter-cultural Cynic and Stoic philosophers. Even in the church's successful fourth and subsequent centuries, extant family traditions were resistant to Christian reforms. The monastic option, for instance, was strategically utilized by the elite classes to keep their family estates intact by sending their daughters to convents and their younger sons to monasteries, thus avoiding costly multiple dowries. However, the transformation of normative marriage and family patterns among these classes necessitated protracted warfare on the part of the ecclesiastical authorities against the prevailing abuses of family patriarchs. Ultimately, coincident with emergent Papal civil authority, the church began to succeed in reshaping the marriage practices of European society and eventually assumed the powers of legitimization for marriage.

Before examining the influence of Christianity on the ancient family, it may be instructive to review the family policy efforts of one of the West's consummate political adepts, Augustus Caesar (27 B.C.E.–14 C.E.).

AUGUSTUS: FAILED IMPERIAL FAMILY POLICY

While many today question both the propriety and potential efficacy of legislating morality, particularly with respect to matters of private life, many Romans, including the brilliant Emperor Augustus, firmly believed that it was obligatory for the government to guide the morals of its people and punish violators.[1] According to an older Roman moral code, it was a duty of the citizen to marry and bear children so to replenish the ranks of Roman citizenry as well as to obtain legitimate heirs to inherit estates.[2]

Around 100 B.C.E., the Romans discovered romantic love with the result that young men, especially from the Roman nobility and the Italian gentry, began to look upon the traditional values associated with respectable marriage and fatherhood with contempt.[3] Also in the last generation of the Roman Republic young women of the Roman aristocracy adopted these same new morals and became known "…for their divorces, their adulteries, and their reluctance to bear children."[4] Augustus sought to defend against this threat to Roman traditional morality arising in the upper classes and, in 29 B.C.E., introduced a law to penalize celibacy and require respectable marriages. However, the opposition was fierce enough to force the astute young politician to withdraw the proposal. The poet Propertius railed against this proposed legislation in an elegy addressed to his beloved Cynthia. "Why should I provide sons to win triumphs for Rome? No, no one of my blood will serve as a soldier…you mean everything to me, Cynthia, more even than having children and continuing my line." (Propertius 2.7.13-14 and 14-20)

Ten years passed until Augustus, now with substantially greater political control having assumed the role of "supervisor of morals" in 18 B.C.E., introduced a series of moral reforms.

This new reform program included the law on adultery and a second ordinance: "To encourage marriage by members of the various classes of citizens." Finally, in 9 C.E., a third law affecting marriage was enacted. These three acts were the basis of Augustus' marriage legislation which remained in effect for three centuries until Constantine.[5] This legislation made marriage a duty incumbent on all Roman men between twenty-five and sixty years of age and all Roman women between twenty-five and fifty. Widowed and divorced persons within these age limits were required to remarry. However, citizens having met their quota of at least three children for a free-born person, and at least four for a freed person, were exempted. Severe fiscal penalties were associated with the Augustan marriage laws, affecting everyone of significant wealth. Augustus' marriage laws were intended to promote the agrarian morality of the Italian hinterlands over that of the urban sophisticates. As might be expected, Augustus' family policy was to little effect. Instead religion was to become, over the long haul, a more powerful agency in transforming the private lives of the Roman people and their descendants.

JESUS AND PAUL ON THE FAMILY

A. Jesus: A Unique View of Marriage: Life-Long Monogamous Commitment

The Hebrew Bible (Old Testament) is both a record of the practices and attitudes of the Israelite people as well as a holy scripture that guided the behavior of this people. These writings tell us much about ancient Hebrew family life. The importance of children, and especially of the male heir, is made abundantly clear in the story of Abraham. His wife, Sarah, offers her handmaiden, Hagar, to him to bring forth a male heir, Ishmael, who is displaced only after Sarah is able to conceive and give birth to Isaac. Both the practices of polygamy and "Levirate marriage" (requiring a man, regardless of his own marital status, to marry his brother's widow when the deceased leaves no children) are rationalized because of the necessity of producing heirs. There are indications early on of a monogamous disposition among the Hebrews. This disposition gradually asserts itself and, becoming dominant, ultimately leads to the virtual disappearance of polygamy among Jews in the Middle Ages. All women and men, including Israelite priests, were expected to marry at an early age, shortly after puberty.[6] The parents, above all the father, played the central role in the selection of spouses for the children, although there is evidence that an exceptionally willful son or even daughter (Genesis 24:8) might successfully resist parental persuasion. No doubt, however, in the overwhelming majority of cases the father's will prevailed in the selection of a bride for his son. Indeed, these writings unequivocally demonstrate that the Hebrew family type was patriarchal in nature. The bridegroom's father paid a "bride price" finalizing the transaction in which the bride joined the bridegroom's family. A further feature of the early Hebrew marriages was instant divorce effected simply by the husband telling the wife to leave.[7] At a later date, the formal procedure was set in place as indicated in Deuteronomy 24:1, whereby the husband is required to "write her a bill of divorce" stating the grounds before expelling her from his house.

Within this Hebraic context, the teachings of Jesus on marriage can only appear as quite extraordinary or even revolutionary. When confronted with the Mosaic allowance for men to divorce their wives, Jesus characterized the Deuteronomic law as a concession: "For your hardness of heart he wrote you this commandment" (Mark 10:5). At the same time Jesus reaches back into the Hebrew tradition identifying the origins of marriage in the divine purpose of creation: "God made them male and female" (Genesis 1:27 and 5:2). Elizabeth Schussler-Fiorenza has correctly pointed to Jesus' use of Genesis 1:27 in Mark 10:7; "For this reason a man shall leave his father and mother and be joined to his wife, and the two shall become one flesh."[8] Here, the man is called upon to sever his connection with his own patriarchal family rather than the woman being handed over to the power of man. Moreover, Jesus' admonition against divorce further emphasizes the notion of husband and wife as equal partners; this is true even though the latter part of the saying is inapplicable to women in Palestine who did not have the right to divorce their husbands: "Whoever divorces his wife and marries another, commits adultery against her; and if she divorces her husband or marries another, she commits adultery."[9]

The radical nature of Jesus' teachings on marriage and divorce can readily be seen by the rapidity of the church's backsliding on the issue of the male right of divorce. Writing some four decades after the death of Jesus, the author of the Gospel of Matthew revises the original saying of Jesus in Mark by allowing the man the right to divorce his wife "for unchastity" (Matthew 19:9). The Markan Jesus saying, in denying divorce equally to husbands and wives, is the more progressive as it flaunts the culturally unquestioned double standard of the time. This crucial exception in the Gospel of Matthew seeks to place Jesus in such respectable Jewish company as the celebrated teacher Shammai (50 B.C.E.-30 C.E.). Shammai held to the same such exception against the equally renowned contemporary, Hillel, who taught that the man may divorce his wife whenever he so wishes. However, both Shammai and Matthew are far less offensive to male marital prerogatives, for it was often relatively easy for dissatisfied husbands to gain a sympathetic audience for his accusations against a wife's infidelity. Thus, as we shall see later in this chapter, only the uncompromising position against divorce of Jesus in Mark will provide the leverage to challenge the historical inequality of women in marital unions.

The central point of Jesus' understanding of marriage is its theocentric origin. Both Mark and Matthew affirm that marriage is an expression of divine intention: "What therefore God has joined together, let no man put asunder."

It should be noted that Jesus is unique among the founders of the major world religions in advocating marriage as a lifelong monogamous commitment.[10]

By placing the authority of marriage beyond all earthly institutions, including those of the patriarchal family and religion, Jesus proclaims a new standard of marital fidelity which both husbands and wives are enjoined to honor.

Jesus' revaluation of the marital relationship is also consonant with his radical reassessment of children, the poor, and such social untouchables as prostitutes and the Samaritans, a despised ethnic and religious minority of first century Palestine. Jesus' mandate for the individual to be concerned with one's own purity of heart rather than the shortcomings of the other (Matthew 5:27; 7:1-5) provides the impetus to ameliorate the conditions of family life and to reduce the mortality of children in ancient and medieval civilizations. In Jesus' "new family of equal discipleship," the little child becomes a primary recipient of the community's care and service (Mark 9:35-37; Matthew 18:1-4 and Luke 9:48). Accordingly, the early Christian Church quickly developed institutions of social welfare for its baptized children and widows that would distinguish it favorably in the

eyes of even otherwise critical Romans. Further, while
Deuteronomy 21:18-21 gives parents the right to hand over a
rebellious son so that "all the men of the city shall stone him to
death," Jesus emphasizes in the parable of the prodigal son the
loving forgiveness of a father towards the son who has squandered
his inheritance.

The challenge of Jesus' familial ethics, however, has never
been fully met by the civilizations upon which it has been thrust.
A part of the history of this encounter between the Jesus marital
ethic and Western society will be examined throughout the re-
mainder of this book.

B. Paul: An Egalitarian View of Marital Relations

Paul of Tarsus,[11] the self-proclaimed apostle to the Gentiles, was
a highly effective urban missionary and church administrator.
Whereas Jesus and his disciples were rural Palestinians, Paul
brought the gospel of Christ to several provincial capital cities in
the eastern part of the Roman Empire and, shortly before his
death, was planning a major initiative in the West beginning in
Rome. Paul was widely conversant with Hellenistic ethical
thought as well as rhetoric and literary conventions.[12] Recently,
Will Deming has convincingly demonstrated the influence of
Stoic-Cynic moral philosophy on Paul's teachings concerning
marriage and sex.[13] In the first century of the Roman Empire,
the question of whether an individual should assume the obligations resulting from marriage and childbearing was openly de-
bated not only by romanticizing poets, as discussed earlier, but
also by both profound and mediocre philosophers and teachers.
The Cynics and Stoics were the two philosophical schools most
deeply engaged in the ancient "battle" over the family and they
took diametrically opposed positions. The Stoics initially were
pro-marriage because they saw it as vital to the well-being of the

city-state. Responsible married life was essential to the healthy household, the basic unit of the city-state. The Stoics further favored marriage, as married life and procreation were necessary for human beings to live in accord with nature, the defining criterion of the good life in Stoic ethics. Taking an opposite position, the Cynics argued that by escaping marriage individuals preserved the free time essential to pursue philosophy and to attain a virtuous life. Deming notes certain Stoics developed a hybrid position wherein they argued that in the presence of special or adverse social circumstances, such as war or poverty, individuals should forgo marriage to pursue the philosophical life. Paul's own position in First Corinthians may be closest to this hybrid Stoic view.

The seventh chapter of First Corinthians contains some of the most often quoted early Christian words on marriage and sex: "To the unmarried and the widows I say that it is well for them to remain unmarried as I am. But if they are not practicing self-control, they should marry. For it is better to marry than to be aflame with passion." (vv. 8-9) At best, this and several other verses in chapter seven including v. 38 "So then, he who marries his fiancee does well; and he who refrains from marriage will do better," would seem to confer a begrudging second class citizenship on married Christians: marriage is only for those who lack self-control. Indeed, such a negative valuation of marriage and sexuality from the second century onwards will be affirmed by much of Christianity.

The problem is that such a rendering of Paul's view neglects several other important elements of the apostle's conception of marriage and sexuality. Paul makes it clear, for example, that his admonitions against marriage derive from his eschatological conviction that the end time is near: "Yet those who marry will experience distress in this life, and I would spare you that. I mean, brothers and sisters, the appointed time has grown short…For the present form of this world is passing away." (vv. 28, 29 and 31b) It is this apocalyptic element that is decisive in Paul's advice concerning the issue of assuming the responsibilities of marriage and family. Given the present "adverse circumstances," Paul recommends against marriage so as to avoid the burden that will distract the devotee from attending to the "affairs of the Lord" in what, from his understanding, are the final moments of fallen history.

Further, Paul, in the opening verses of chapter seven, opposes extreme sexual asceticism in the Corinthian community. He advises husbands and wives *not* to withhold conjugal rights from each other (v. 3) "except perhaps by agreement for a set time" (v. 5). Paul's advice reflects an egalitarian view of the relationship between husband and wife, especially with respect to sexual relationships: "For the wife does not have authority over her own body, but the husband does; likewise the husband does not have authority over his own body, but the wife does" (v.4). There is nothing squeamish here about Paul's advice on sex to the married couple. The anonymous letter to the Hebrews, transmitted as part of the Pauline correspondence by the early church, pronounces: "Let marriage be held in honor by all, and let the marriage bed be kept undefiled" (13:49). The later First Timothy, pseudonymously attributed to Paul, explicitly condemns Gnostic heretics who "forbid marriage and demand abstinence from foods" (4:3). Earlier in the same letter, the conditions set forth for those aspiring to the office of Bishop include that the candidate be the "husband of one wife" and "manage his household well" (3:4). Nevertheless, the ascetic and celibate tendencies consciously subdued in the Pauline and Deutero-Pauline tradition soon take center stage in church history.

DEMOCRATIZING ELITIST SEXUAL IDEALS: CELIBACY AND THE POWER TO CHANGE SOCIETY

Spanning the second to the fourth centuries, an array of articulate Christian spokespersons directed their rhetoric not only at the emperors and all other outsiders, but also inwardly toward each other, as they often vehemently disagreed about the meaning of the gospels. Such intra-Christian polemics were particularly intense with respect to questions of marriage and celibacy.[14] Although they represented widely diverse constituencies and perspectives, two major groups, known as the "Gnostics" and the "Catholics," emerged in the second century. The Gnostics embraced a radical dualism that denied value not only to the material realm, but also to the "God" who created this material world. For the Gnostics, both marriage and procreation were part of the evil empire that evolved as a consequence of the fall of Adam and Eve. Catholics, on the other hand, acknowledged marriage and procreation as good, even though most tended to affirm celibacy, or at least "chaste marriage," as a spiritually higher way of life. Justin, while calling attention to the sexual excesses of the Roman gods, people, and even past emperors[15], proudly flaunts before his addressees, the Emperors Antoninus Pius and Marcus Aurelius, the admirable self-restraint of Christians who engage in sex only to procreate. One's sense of the extraordinary moral austerity of early Christians can only be enhanced upon recalling that contraception, abortion, the exposure of unwanted infants and the infanticide of slave children were "common and perfectly legal practices."[16] Moreover, there is ample evidence for the sexual use and abuse of both adult and child slaves by wealthy Romans. Christians, despite their internal differences, were widely recognized even by their opponents as exceptionally self-restrained in sexual matters.

Notwithstanding their distinctiveness in lifestyle, early Christian moral teachings were derived in large part from contemporary philosophical thought. Moreover, much of the Christian sexual ethic was not unique—even the restriction of sexual intercourse to the purpose of procreation was a Stoic innovation. Under the influence of the Stoics, the ideals of sexual self-restraint, family responsibility, and the relative equality of husband and wife comprised an elitist tradition that touched a small percentage of the upper classes; included in such a class was the Emperor Marcus Aurelius.

The Christian leaders were able rapidly to democratize these ideals of sexual self-restraint leading, in the words of Peter Brown, to the "*most* profound single revolution of the late classical period."[17] Thus, through Christian preaching and writings, relatively rarefied philosophical notions of private spiritual life reached thousands of the more humble classes. From Paul onward, the Christian movement was, in terms of class, a relatively diversified movement extensive with the social stratification of the wider Roman society. Unlike Judaism, which offered its followers clear ritual boundaries through circumcision and dietary laws, Christians differentiated themselves from the pagan world in large part by adhering to an exceptional sexual discipline. Christians rejected divorce and disapproved of the remarriage of widows. They practiced a marital ethic that followed the highest ideals of Roman morality.

The Christian's sexual self-discipline impacted not only their personal lives but also their institutional existence. Christian young people married early in order to avoid the temptations of illicit sexual liaisons, especially with non-Christians. By avoiding remarriage, the community could be assured of a supply of mature individuals able to devote their energies to the service of the church.[18] Celibacy became the price of access to leadership in the Christian community; during the ancient period celibacy primarily took the form of postmarital abstinence, adopted usually in middle age.

The early church effectively redirected Christians' libidinal energies towards the work of social service. The tradition of caring for children and the poor, dating back to the earliest church, was critical in reinforcing the solidarity of the Christian community and, as I will explain, was pivotal in its eventual success in gaining a privileged status in the Roman Empire. In 248, the Church of Rome had a staff of 155 clergy supporting fifteen hundred widows and poor in addition to the regular congregation. This was an enormous organization by contemporary Roman standards when the average religious community or voluntary association numbered in the scores, not in hundreds.[19]

It is probably impossible to discern the sincerity of Constantine's "conversion to Christianity" in 312. Certainly most of the extant contemporaneous sources were authored by Christian admirers, the tone of whose literary efforts on the topic approach the pious biographies of church saints. In any case, as an emperor whose career proved him to be one of the more ambitious among his peers, Constantine was probably equally impressed with the effectiveness of the alternative society which Christians had constructed, particularly given the seemingly irreversible decline of the wealthy class of patrons responsible for the welfare of the Roman cities. The Christian community exhibited the will to order and public consciousness that would appeal to an emperor wishing to shore up his own crumbling infrastructure, while at the same time facing unrelenting attacks from the Germanic tribes and the Persians, who for centuries had both been enduring threats to the empire.[20] For our pur-

poses, it is important to examine how the Christian understanding of the family and sexuality shaped, and was shaped by, the
impressive emerging Christian organization.

In the fourth century, the Bishop was powerful politically,
economically, and spiritually; his prestige was based on his ability to care for multitudes of poor in the Christian congregation.
As at the time of Paul, not all Christians were poor; a significant
group of influential women, mostly widows and virgins, supported the Bishop's efforts on behalf of the poor. The Bishop
directed these womens' energies and wealth in service of the
church, and in turn protected them when necessary from exploitation by the male-oriented Roman system. Most importantly, Catholic Christianity had now ingeniously discovered the
path to turn the reserved energies and resources of those forsak-
ing sexuality to the support of beleaguered families. Catholic
celibates would traverse this path again and again through the
centuries in order to come to the aid of those in need.

The Christian movement fulfilled a deep psychological need
for order and self-control. In particular, it offered a rationale for
controlling the sex drive. Augustine pointed to the swamping of
the conscious mind in orgasm for both men and women as evidence of the symptoms of original sin.[21] In his final theological
dispute with Pelagius, Augustine argued that sexual desire and
death are essentially "unnatural" experiences resulting from the
sin of Adam and Eve.[22] Whereas earlier representatives of Christian Orthodoxy, including Justin, Ireneus, Tertullian, Clement
and Origen, affirmed the human person's moral freedom to control one's life, including sexual life, Augustine denied the descendants of sinful Adam and Eve the free will and capacity to
live in accord with God's will. The best one can do is to gain a
battlefield advantage by abandoning the "world" and retreating

to a monastic setting. Although the majority of Christians married, most Christians affirmed the primacy of renunciation. When Jovian, himself a celibate monk, argued that celibate persons are no holier than those who marry, he was attacked by the most prestigious Christian authorities of his time, including Jerome, Ambrose and Augustine. Indeed in 392, he was excommunicated by Pope Siricius, Bishop of Rome.[23] The notion that the celibate way was spiritually higher than the married way was firmly, some may argue indelibly, imprinted in the Catholic consciousness.

During the century following the conversion of Constantine, the number of Christians grew from about five million to thirty million.[24] Unlike the Christians of prior times, there was no longer an instant social penalty to be paid upon being recognized as a disciple of Christ; rather Christian identity now conferred preferential treatment. No doubt, many so-called Christians had mixed motives and lived their lives with far less distinctiveness from the pagans than had been the case in the previous era. Perhaps it was precisely this scenario that made Augustine's more pessimistic view of human nature and politics so compelling to leaders of the post-Constantinian Church.

Certainly those more religiously inclined continued to find their place within the expanded church. In this same century of rapid growth, Christians seeking high-intensity religion would and did opt for the monastic life; there were some thirty thousand monks in Egypt alone during this time. In effect the disparity once found between Christians and the wider society, especially with respect to sexual and family practices, was now to be found within the confines of the church. It would take centuries more for Christianity to begin to domesticate men who were the heads of vast numbers of nominal-believer households in the Holy Roman Empire.

THE CHURCH BEGINS TO TRANSFORM MARITAL NORMS AND EXPECTATIONS: THE INDISSOLUBILITY OF MARRIAGE

The Franks, a group of Germanic tribes, were held in check by Roman legions for more than two centuries until 486, when Clovis took possession of Gaul and expelled the last Roman governor. Ten years later, Clovis converted to Christianity at the prompting of his wife; thereafter a close relationship between the Frankish rulers and the Papacy was initiated.

What were the characteristics of Frankish family life? According to Tacitus, the men of Germanic tribes were unique among the barbarians in that they lived with only one wife. Because women did most of the productive work, such as farming, a husband provided a dowry to his wife. Traditionally, wives apparently accompanied their husbands to the battlefield where they tended their wounds as well as fed them. Within the confines of the Roman empire, however, Frankish wives became more domesticated and were left at home on such forays. When Clovis ascended to power, he opened the door to direct Christian influence on the Frankish family.[25] Over a period of centuries, this influence was to have profound impact on Western standards and expectations with respect to family life.

Around the time Clovis was establishing his kingdom, the churchman, Caesarius of Arles, was sermonizing against the hypocrisy of men who, expecting fidelity from their spouses, indulged freely their own sexual whims.[26] Also, while the church's impact on the ruling classes' familial practices is quite limited throughout the Merovingian period, beginning with Clovis, Caesarius and other church leaders encouraged women to pursue monastic vocations which offered them varying degrees of independence from male domination. Caesarius also objected to the widespread practice among the nobility of procuring their wives through abduction and as victor's booty. When the Franks defeated the Thuringian king in 531 and captured his daughter Radegard, the sons of Clovis contested her hand in a judicial battle.[27] Desirable women were commonly abducted and were married to their abductors against both their wishes and, more consequentially, the wishes of their fathers. Given that the crux of Merovingian society was strong kinship groups, revenge was often taken directly by the blood relatives of the abductee. The chronicles record that Saint Rictrud's brothers killed her husband several years after her abduction, even though by that time several children had been born of the union.[28]

Merovingian kings readily granted their most trusted servants permission to abduct girls from wealthy families. Ecclesiastical authorities opposed the Merovingians on this score and passed its own legislation encouraging women fearing abduction to take refuge in the church. Not until 614, at the Council of Paris, did a Merovingian king renounce the practice of his predecessors, ordering capital punishment for the abductors of women relatives.[29] It would take several centuries, however, before the church's position on this matter would fully prevail in the wider society.

The church also opposed incestuous marriages, a practice quite widely followed by the wealthy in order to protect their possessions and strengthen kinship bonds. As in its opposition to abduction, the church argued that marriage should promote the cause of peace and that exogamous unions better served this end as they linked together the fractious kin groups of society. By the end of the sixth century, the church's firm stand against incest was becoming effective, making it difficult for kings to disregard the prohibition without consequence. Nevertheless, in the Merovingian period (481-751) the marriage laws and practices of Frankish society were in general far distant from the Christian ideal of lifelong monogamy and coincided explicitly only in the former's condemnation of abortion, abduction and female unchastity.[30] Four Merovingian kings indulged in polygynous unions; among other kings concubinage was rampant. Suzanne Wemple aptly characterizes the state of Merovingian marriage ethics: "The combination of Germanic polygamy and the Roman institution of concubinage gave almost complete license to men to be promiscuous, furthered male dominance, and accentuated sexual double standards in Merovingian society."[31] It was not until the rise of the Carolingian kings (751-987) that the church would begin to transform the accepted standards of family ethics.

In Carolingian times, the indissolubility of marriage became a central issue. The insistence by the church on the binding nature of marriage had both profound moral as well as social significance in Frankish and in European society. The initial impetus to embrace the reform ideas concerning sexual relations advocated by Saint Boniface and other church leaders may have been largely political. As usurpers of the throne, the Carolingians needed ecclesiastical sanction for their new dynasty. Pepin, founder of the Carolingian Dynasty, also saw in St. Boniface's reform platform a weapon against "the widespread networks of alliances among the great families, which was formed mainly through marriages."[32] Noting that incest remained unchecked among the Frankish nobility, St. Boniface enlisted the support of popes in prohibiting the practice. Pepin also readily joined the campaign by promulgating the incest prohibitions as part of his royal enactments. Pepin embraced less than wholeheartedly, however, Boniface's views on the indissolubility of marriage; these views precluded second or third unions while a previous partner was still alive. With Pepin presiding, the 757 Council of Compiègne stressed that both men and women were subject to the same laws. At the Council of Verberie (758-768) Pepin allowed divorce and remarriage "in the case of a man whose wife had tried to kill him or refused to follow him."[33]

Charlemagne was more strict than his father, Pepin, in upholding Christian morality. In 789, Charlemagne prohibited the remarriage of any divorced man or woman. Further, in 796 Charlemagne proclaimed that "adultery could not dissolve the marriage bond."[34] Although a cuckolded husband could separate from his wife, he could not remarry while she lived. In 802, two years after his coronation as emperor of the Holy Roman Empire, Charlemagne extended this legislation to the entire Frankish Empire.

Charles' own life may give some insight into how at least some of the royalty and nobility coped with these stringent measures. Before his legislation on the indissolubility of marriage, Charles divorced twice in his youth; he lived steadfastly, however, with each of his next three wives until their deaths.[35] After the death of his fifth wife in 800, Charlemagne did not remarry but enjoyed the company of four concubines. Nevertheless, the distance between Frankish customs and Christian ideals of marriage had been reduced.

Louis the Pious, Charlemagne's only surviving son and his successor, was more ardent in pursuing these ideals both personally and in his role as ruler of the empire. He prevented bastards from succession to the throne and linked legitimacy to the validity of the parents' marriage.[36] After the death of his first wife, Louis married Judith who was thereafter accused of adultery; the King nevertheless refused to divorce her. This instance suggests that by this time, the principle of marital indissolubility was widely accepted.

In 846 and 847, bishops meeting at Meaux and Paris warned women and men to guard against adultery, concubinage and incest. With the exception of the principle of marital indissolubility and the prohibition against incest the church, in the second half of the ninth century, after Louis, the bishops accommodated secular customs.

Yet Christianity had clearly distinguished the characteristics of an ecclesiastical model of marriage from the prevailing lay model. Although abductions, repudiation of wives and violation of incest laws continued, in the course of the next three centuries, the ideals now enshrined in secular as well as ecclesiastical legislation would come to be accepted in the popular consciousness of Western Europe, thereby setting new public expectations for marriage and family. Most importantly, the emphasis on the indissolubility of marriage elevated the status of the wife, preparing the way for the conjugal family as the basic unit of society, and displacing the extended family as the dominant form of social organization.[37]

THE SACRALIZATION OF MARRIAGE: THE NEW STATUS QUO OF THE FAMILY

A gradual process of sacralizing marriage began in Carolingian France (751-987) and was not culminated until the thirteenth century. In 860, the Archbishop of Reims, Hincmar, loudly protested King Lothair II's (the grandson of Louis the Pious) repudiation of his wife in favor of a preferred woman. In the centuries following that of Louis the Pious, such practices, as well as that of marrying near kin and of abduction, continued, as testified to

by numerous condemnatory treatises of churchmen.[38] Moreover, marriage remained within the jurisdiction of civil law; priests
were not closely involved in the marriage ceremony except in
the case of queens.[39]

Yet Hincmar and others like him were ready to stand stead-
fast for the evangelical law of one sole wife, and against abduction and marriage within the seventh degree of blood kinship.
The church mounted its campaign against abduction and incest
(in the wide interpretation just mentioned) on the grounds that
they violated the peace of society by setting families seeking revenge for wrong done to their kin in conflict with the wrongdo-
ers. Sound and wholesome marriage principles would expand
the realm of amity and promote the peace and welfare of society,
argued the ecclesiastical reformers who sought to transform the
church as well as the wider society.

Around the year 1000, the church was able to crystallize its
position on marriage, effecting greater clarity in its own rulings
and demonstrating its authority over family practices of even
the royalty. The Christianization of marriage practices was more
readily accomplished among the lower classes, and the church's
version of marriage quickly replaced concubinage.[40]

King Robert of France and King Henry of Germany, at the
beginning of the eleventh century, were to provide the church
an opportunity to exhibit its influence upon royal marital choices
and practices. Having been brought up by churchmen, and as a
friend to the great monastic reformers of his time, including
Abbot Odilon of Cluny, Henry waited until his twenty-third
year to marry, taking as his bride a member of the lower ranks of
the nobility so as to avoid "incest." Henry, who was caught up
in the millenarian movement of his day, sought to restore order
and peace to the world and also to purify God's people. Believ-

ing that he himself should be a model for a new purified people, Henry refused to repudiate his wife, Cunegonde, although their union was fruitless. In biographies written after their death, the church portrayed the couple as living in absolute conjugal chastity and departing this world as virgins. Such literary inventions served the purposes of more austere ecclesiastical reformers at the end of the eleventh century.

Between 1007 and 1012, Bourchard of Worms drew up a collection of texts known as the *Decretum* that was to have enormous influence on marital practices in Germany, Italy and France. This *Decretum* devoted considerable attention to marriage; more than a quarter of its text dealt with marriage and fornication. Promoting monogamy was its primary objective; prohibitions and punishments were much more relaxed for those not yet married. The *Decretum* condemned adultery by either sex, but urged husbands to forgive adulterous wives, noting that women were reluctant to accuse their husbands while men habitually hauled their wives before priests with such charges. The most severe punishment was meted out for bestiality, abduction and adultery. Bourchard could be lenient towards the sexual escapades of unmarried men, but abduction and adultery were harshly condemned. He was, after all, more concerned with order and peace and less so with cleansing society of sin.[41] Bourchard still remained flexible with respect to indissolubility, allowing Bishops to dissolve unions other than those deemed incestuous by the church. The *Decretum* granted less discretion to bishops in permitting those they had allowed to separate to marry again while their former partner was still alive. Bourchard's *Decretum*, offering the most comprehensive compendium of ecclesiastical marital regulations, informed church leaders as they guided the family life of the faithful. The great masses of people began to adjust their way of marrying in accord with emerging church traditions.

The church's influence over family life, especially royal marital practices, was still rather limited. The case of Robert the "pious" illustrates this point. Unopposed by local bishops, King Robert pursued a trigamous relationship, thus indicating how tenuous a hold, even at the beginning of the eleventh century, the ecclesiastical model of marriage had on the European nobility. The Council of Rome, however, perhaps equally disturbed by the fact that Robert's third wife was connected to him by blood, intervened and Robert was anathematized by the Pope. Later, when his wife bore him a deformed child, Robert "got" religion and repudiated her. The church exploited this "submission" and presented Robert as the repentant, pious sovereign. Bishops continued to care for repudiated women, exhorted their husbands to take them back, and refused to give such husbands permission to remarry.

During the tenth and eleventh centuries, as the feudalization of Europe proceeded, great families adopted the practice of deciding upon a sole successor/heir in each generation; thus emerged the monarchical rule of powerful patriarchs. This sole male was in control of the wealth of the family and was responsible for arranging marriages for his children and the children of his sisters. By allowing perhaps only one of his sons legitimate marriage the family estate was kept intact, concentrating and centralizing wealth in the hands of a few feudal lords. This concentration of wealth was furthered by a change occurring somewhat before the mid-eleventh century which excluded women from control over family property. Coinciding with the emergence of great families, the church was winning its long fought battle for clerical celibacy. In this struggle, it enjoyed the support of the heads of the great families who, interested in limiting the number of claimants to inheritance, had paid to stow away many of their younger relatives in monasteries to prevent them from begetting legitimate children.

From another quarter, heretics attacked the church's involvement in the sacramentalizing of marriage, arguing that it was utterly inappropriate to pronounce a blessing on physical unions. In order to stave off arch heretics while it continued to pursue its agenda of reforming the laity primarily through fostering life-long monogamous marriages, the church established a "pure", celibate priesthood and thus sought to blunt the heretic's criticism of the church's moral laxity. As the church, in the course of the eleventh century, succeeded in imposing punishment upon such public crimes as adultery and abduction, it *de facto* came to displace the secular authorities in such matters. In the last decades of the eleventh century, the reforming prelates even attacked the most prominent nobles in their relentless efforts to transform the marital practices of the laity. Pope Urban II and Yves of Chartres, for example, condemned the King of France, Philip I, who abducted the wife of a count, his cousin, and lived with her while his first wife was still alive.

Also during this period, the custom of involving a priest in engagement as well as nuptial ceremonies became fixed. A priest was also involved in the blessing of the ring before the mass as well as the blessing of the wedding chamber. These ceremonies effectively constituted a sacralization of marriage and thus reinforced the church's moral influence upon Western marital practices.

2

The Recovery of Adam's Helpmate: The Rise of Companionate Marriage

In the church's first thousand or so years, its primary impact on the social life of the family can best be characterized as the curtailment of male abuses of women and children. The sacralization of marriage, the affirmation of the indissolubility of the marital union and the imposition of ecclesiastical sanctions against men, especially the wealthy, who abandoned their spouses for more attractive quarry, protected the only social status available to women of the time, that of wife. Meanwhile, the church still performed the role of protecting women from violent husbands who tended to resolve their marital problems through brute force. Later, in the course of the 800 years from 1200 to the twentieth century, Christianity would contribute centrally to the domestication of men and to what historians and sociologists have termed "the feminization of the family."[1] In this period, the roles of husbands and wives and their expectations of each other would change gradually and then dramatically, as would, as we shall see in the following chapter, the roles and mutual expectations of parents and children.

THOMAS AQUINAS: MARRIAGE AS FRIENDSHIP BETWEEN EQUALS

The greatest Christian medieval theologian, Thomas Aquinas (1225-1274), unsurprisingly affirmed the indissolubility of marriage, thus denying husbands the right to repudiate their wives. His reasons, in support of the church's position, foreshadow the long rise of the ideal of companionate marriage. Thomas describes the relationship between husband and wife as one of the "greatest friendship" which arises from not only their unity "in the act of fleshly union" but also from their "partnership of the whole range of domestic activity."[2] Given the historic inaccessibility of divorce to wives, Thomas argues that husbands should not be allowed to abandon them, for otherwise "the society of husband and wife would not be an association of equals, but instead a sort of slavery on the part of the wife."[3] Thomas also appeals to the argument that friendship requires equality in his criticism of polygamy: "for a man to have several wives,…the friendship of wife for husband would not be free, but somewhat servile; and this argument is corroborated by experience, for among husbands having plural wives, the wives have a status like that of servants."[4] Thus, lifelong monogamous marriage becomes the precondition for the "friendship of equals" in which husband and wife are to participate. Fond of naturalistic arguments, Thomas affirms that for any man to take a woman in the time of her youth, beauty, and fecundity and then to send her away in her advanced years, would violate a natural law of equity or justice.

Thomas' biological orientation led him to a more favorable opinion of coitus than his predecessor Augustine.[5] Carnal union cannot be evil in itself, according to Thomas, because it is the very purpose of the sexual bodily organs. Further, he argues that the fact that all animals have a natural inclination for carnal union means it is good. The most important natural fact negating the notion that sexual union is inherently evil is that procreation requires it.

For Thomas, Augustine and the later Protestant reformers, original sin caused a disordering of the affections so that humans do not love in accordance with "right reason," which requires the highest good to be given the greatest love. As a result of the fall, the rational and the conscious is overwhelmed by the emotional and unconscious, a phenomenon that is especially the case in the moment of orgasm. But with Thomas, the good of the rational order is given a new importance in Christianity. The scientific writings of Aristotle, reintroduced into the West via Islam, find a central place in Christian thought through Thomas Aquinas' theological writings. Aristotle argued that pleasure itself, an entirely natural response, was neither good nor evil: only intentional acts have ethical significance. Any pleasure derived from such acts was either good or bad in accordance with the moral quality of the intentions in question.[6] Consequently, Thomas reasoned that because intercourse in marriage was a legitimate act, the pleasure produced by that act entailed not even venial sin. Thomas' assertions of a fundamental equality between husband and wife, as well as the natural and thus good character of marital intercourse, would come to have a direct influence on the West's understanding of marriage, paving the way for the companionate ideal.

ERASMUS: WOMAN AS AN INTELLECTUAL AND SPRITUAL PARTNER TO MAN

Erasmus (1469-1536), the culminating voice of the Renaissance, articulates the changing spiritual estimation of marriage as well as an elevated understanding of woman as wife. In 1523, Erasmus published five colloquies on various aspects of love and marriage. In the dialogue entitled *Courtship*, Maria shows herself to be more rational, philosophical and a better disputant than her suitor, Pamphilus. Indeed, Pamphilus admits to loving her mind more than Maria's physical beauty, for her mind's beauty "will forever increase with age."[7] Similarly in Erasmus' dialogue, *The Girl With No Interest In Marriage*, Catharine is praised by her male interlocutor as "blessed with a wit worthy of your beauty" and adds, "I wish I had your aptitude for the liberal arts."[8]

The appearance, during the Renaissance, of a view of woman as an intellectual is an important corollary to the emerging reinterpretation of marriage as more than an alternative for the incontinent's life of sin. Indeed, it is a necessary precondition for the rise of the companionship rationale for marriage, which Erasmus hints is even more important than the procreative justification for marriage.[9] Only as woman becomes recognized as an intellectual and spiritual partner to man can the companionate ideal take hold. Most ancient and medieval thinkers described woman as more materialistic, earthy and of weaker mind than man.

Erasmus also presages the radical reversal of the relative assessments of the spiritual capacity of men and women which, as we shall see, will be realized by American Christianity of the nineteenth century. In his dialogue entitled *Marriage*, where two married women are in conversation, Erasmus makes it clear that he is aware that marriages of his day are not egalitarian partnerships. Nevertheless, the more mature Christian, Eulalia, counsels her younger friend, a newlywed, to domesticate her husband "as do those who tame elephants and lions or suchlike creatures that can't be forced."[10] Later, she refers to trainers of horses who use calls, whistles, caresses and "other means of soothing mettlesome animals" and reflects "How much more fitting for us to use those arts on our husbands with whom, whether we like it or not, we share bed and board for our entire lives."[11] The depiction of the husband as the more bestial to be tamed by his wife may not be surprising to the modern reader, but is striking in the historical context of prior and contemporary literature. There can be little doubt that patriarchs still reigned in the family, but there are the beginnings of the recognition of a more influential position that women may occupy within the family because of their greater spiritual acumen.

Erasmus, in both his personal life as well as his writings, expressed criticism of the monastic lifestyle and seemed at times explicitly to esteem married life above that of celibacy. As a youth, Erasmus had been sent to an Augustinian monastery; thereafter, he left the monastery and his failure to return was legally the equivalent of military desertion. In 1517, however, Erasmus received a Papal dispensation permitting him to live in the world, which he had already been doing for over twenty years.

Favoring the marital state, Erasmus is critical of the moral lapses of monks and nuns. In the dialogue *The Repentant Girl,* Catharine's male friend congratulates her on her decision to leave the convent. He had earlier urged her not to commit herself to the convent and instead "to marry a husband of similar tastes and establish a new community at home. Your husband would be father of it, you the mother."[12] In another dialogue, Erasmus admonishes the convent-bound Catharine: "you have Christ at home as well."[13]

Although Erasmus does not quite deny the spiritual superiority of celibacy as compared to marriage, he does believe few possess a genuine call for the celibate life, and those without the gift of continence are prone to the hypocritical monastic excesses which he satirizes in so many of his writings. Like later

Reformers, Erasmus sees the moral failings of much of late medieval Christianity, but unlike the Protestant Reformers, he was not willing to sever his relationship with the Roman Catholic Church.

THE REFORMATION: MARRIAGE MORE PLEASING TO GOD THAN CELIBACY

Like their Renaissance counterparts, the leaders of the Protestant Reformation attacked in writings as well as from their pulpits that which they perceived to be the anti-marriage celibate ideal of Catholicism.[14] The activist religious reformers advocated clerical marriage and many of them, priests and monks, stepped forward to marry. Andreas Karlstadt, after authoring the first Protestant work against celibacy, married in 1521, explaining that he wished to provide a "good model and example" to "miserable and lost clerics."[15] By 1526, most reformers, including Martin Luther, had become husbandly role models. By this time, marriage had become a litmus test of commitment to Protestantism.[16] Not satisfied with merely critiquing monasticism and celibacy as contrary to both "nature and Christian freedom," the Reformers constructed positive justifications for marriage. Reversing Catholic spirituality, the Reformers considered marriage to be far more pleasing to God than celibacy, which had led many clerics to a life of hypocrisy and fornication. On the other hand, marriage provided a way to fulfill natural urgings of the flesh without sinning as well as to be fruitful and increase the church. As we will see later, Puritans and later Protestants were to elaborate greatly on the benefits and blessings of the married state and especially emphasize the duty of husbands and wives to love each other.

As with almost any important historical movement, the Reformation produced several unintended consequences, a few of which were quite significant for the institution of marriage in the West. In rejecting the sacrament of marriage, the Reformers effectively sought to deny the Catholic Church legal jurisdiction over marriage. In so doing, the Reformers unwittingly were to help secularize the institution of marriage and delimit their own potential authority over marriage. As Eric Carlson has observed, in city after city which became aligned with Protestantism in the sixteenth century, the secular courts became responsible for marriage.[17] Carlson mentions Augsburg, Hohenlohe and Nuremberg, among others.

Further, as mentioned earlier, canon law upheld marriages entered into without parental consent; thus, lay elites concerned about maintaining family assets readily joined in the Protestant assault on canon law, especially with respect to marriage. While sharing Protestant distaste for church marriage courts, secular leaders were not eager to transfer matrimonial jurisdiction to the Protestant clergy. Although a long-term consequence of this turn of events may have been the secularization of marriage in the West, a more immediate outcome was the strengthening of patriarchal authority within the family,[18] as the home became a center of religious activity, with the father playing the key role.

THE PURITANS: THE FOUNDING VIEW OF THE AMERICAN FAMILY

A. The English Way

Lawrence Stone has described the type of family which defined domestic life in sixteenth century England thusly: "the family therefore, was an open-ended, low-keyed, unemotional, authoritarian institution which served certain essential political, economic, sexual, procreative and nurturant purposes."[19] The family unit was quite short-lived, frequently dissolved by the death of a husband or wife, or by the death or early departure from the home of children: "So far as the individual members were concerned, it was neither very durable, nor emotionally or sexually very demanding; the closest analogy to a sixteenth century home is a bird's nest."[20] This description would be applicable to the family before the sixteenth century in England as well as, with few modifications, to contemporaneous families in other parts of Europe.

Stone notes also that in the sixteenth century, a new type of family begins to emerge. Whereas in the first type of family the conjugal couple was subordinated, even submerged, within the wider kinship group, the second type was less porous to outside influence and was an increasingly private nuclear family.

Stone allows a significant role to the influence of missionary Protestantism, "especially its Puritan wing," in bringing Christian morality to a majority of gentry and urban bourgeoisie and, thus, in effecting the conditions for this new type of nuclear family.[21] The Puritans, for example, propagated the family as a partial substitute for the parish.[22] To this end, the Protestant doctrine of the priesthood of all believers was effectively translated into a social reality of the husband and father as the spiritual as well as secular head of the household.[23] At the same time, Anglican, especially Puritan, preachers elevated the conjugal bond in sermon after sermon, while singing the praises of holy matrimony.

In 1549, the Archbishop Thomas Cranmer officially added to the Book of Common Prayer, the official service book of the Church of England, a further rationale for marriage beyond the two ancient justifications: the avoidance of fornication and the procreation of legitimate children. Cranmer described the additional rationale as "mutual society, help and comfort that one ought to have of the other, both in prosperity and in adversity."[24] The Puritan Richard Baxter was later to reverse the order of marriage motives as found in the Book of Common Prayer and put mutual comfort and support before procreation.[25] Thus, the Puritans raised the standard as well as the expectations of married love. In addition, the Puritan emphasis on the interior life and individual conscience helped develop the human psychic potential for those more intimate personal relationships which would be necessary to the emergence of the intensive nuclear family. In so doing, however, Puritanism created the opportunity for conflict between the higher expectations for conjugal affection and the demand to obey parental wishes. Puritan theologians proposed that unless acute hostility manifested upon the first meeting, spouses could develop deep and lasting affections after marriage. Paradoxically, it was the Puritan insistence on the divine mandate for conjugal affection that set in motion the historic psychic forces, that joined with changed social and economic conditions, to limit greatly the influence of parents in children's marital decisions. Even the Puritan insistence on subordinating material consideration in marital choices to spiritual concerns was to play its part in reducing parental control in marital choice.

B. Puritans and the First American Families

Ultimately frustrated in their efforts to reform church and state in England, some of the Puritans were to leave England and make it to the shores of New England. Governor Winthrop of the Massachusetts Bay Colony intended, upon his arrival in the new world, to create a model community—a "city on a hill"— whose glory would reflect back to England and accomplish the purification of his beloved homeland from afar. In his famous sermon, "A Model of Christian Charity," Winthrop recommends the "exercise of mutual" love in marriage as a major type of spiritual harmony required in the city on a hill.

Although the Plymouth Puritans came to America only after experiencing frustration in their first land of refuge, Holland, they also sought to manifest in the new world their religious ideals. The enhanced importance of family life for these early European settlers was part and parcel of the English Puritan movement. While there was continuous commerce in ideas between Puritans in old and New England, the Puritans in the new world had, at least for a few decades, the opportunity to create and control the social and institutional structures in accordance with their religious ideals.

1. Affirming the Importance of Marriage as a Spiritual and Carnal Union

Given popular as well as some scholarly views of the Puritans, they would appear to be unlikely candidates for the role of promoting a positive valuation of marriage and family. The word puritanical in common parlance means excessively rigid and austere in religious and moral matters and carries connotations contrary to that of such words as humanistic, intimate and familial. In the popular mind, there is little distinction between the rigors of medieval monasticism and the religious proclivities of the seventeenth-century Puritans.

More troubling is the misunderstanding of Puritanism characteristic of historical sociologists. Edmund Leites has criticized Max Weber's influential description of Puritanism as "ascetic" and "world-rejecting": "In one respect, at least Weber is entirely mistaken. Puritanism has at its very heart an ethic which is world-affirming. In their philosophy of marriage—one of the most important domains of life for Puritanism—preachers and theologians call for spontaneous enjoyment, sexual pleasure, and mutual delight."[26]

While the correctness of Leites' observations is obvious to anyone who has read the plethora of seventeenth-century Puritan handbooks on marriage and family, he offers two possible explanations for the prevalent misunderstanding about the Puritans. The first is related to the historical fact that the heirs of Puritanism, namely the eighteenth- and nineteenth-century English Dissenters and Evangelicals, often did have an unfavorable view of even marital sexuality. This of course is contrary to the Puritans, who saw conjugal love as a "remarkable and happy harmony of carnal, moral, and spiritual bonds."[27] Second, Weber and others have mistaken the Puritan demand for thorough self-discipline with that for sexual renunciation. Accordingly, they have dismissed or overlooked the Puritan view that sexual relations within marriage were not only not confined to procreation, but were also intended to provide comfort and joy, qualities which both expressed and deepened spousal bonds.

In sum, the Puritans argued more consistently and cogently for the spiritual superiority of marriage over celibacy than any movement in the prior history of Christianity. It is reasonable to ask how this biblically grounded community reconciled its view of marriage with the Scriptures.

2. The Bible and the Puritan Family

In his 1634 comprehensive handbook on marriage and the family, *Bethel: A Forme For Families*, Matthew Griffith asserts that all household norms are to be found in the canonical books of the Old and New Testaments.[28] In developing their conduct books for the family, the Puritan writers drew most heavily upon the Old Testament and were especially admiring of Abraham and Rebecca.[29] Griffith states emphatically that "...marriage is in itself a state far more excellent than the single life"[30] and proceeds to Genesis to support this claim. Marriage is preferred to the single state, reasons Griffith, because the former was ordained in Paradise for Adam when he was still innocent. Griffith argues for this from Genesis 4:19, "...the two shall become one flesh," implying that an unmarried man is not complete. For Griffith, this helps to explain the opinion among Jews that "it was ever held reproachful to die a virgin."[31] Griffith will allow a superiority to the single state because, as a result of human sinfulness, the original order has been corrupted. Yet Griffith is quick to point out that the Bible shows that married men have done as much good as unmarried men.[32] He opposes Moses, who was married, to Paul "who may have been married" and affirms that Moses had equal learning, devotion and revelation to that of the latter.[33] Griffith also argues that while the single life may be good, for an unmarried person feeds, clothes and adorns himself, "marriage exceeds in this that he doth good to others."[34]

3. Covenant and Family: Marriage as Divinely Ordained

A comprehensive theological and spiritual rationalization of marriage and the family was first articulated by the Puritans of England and New England in a massive outpouring of writings devoted to the topic between 1620 and 1660. This material possibly equals in volume all Christian literature on marriage for the entire previous fifteen centuries.

According to the Puritans, God instituted marriage before the fall of Adam. Thus, its purpose necessarily preceded and exceeded a traditional Christian view of marriage as an antidote to concupiscence. The Puritans may be the first Christians to fully appreciate marriage as a divinely ordained society in which a full

sharing of the spiritual and sensual dimensions of human existence is made possible. To be sure, the inherent possibilities of
marriage are the result of God's original intention expressed at
the time of the creation of Adam and Eve that they should enjoy
a blessed union. As we shall see later, the New England Puritans'
awareness of the corrupting influence of sin predisposed them
to constructing a society in which laws and government reinforced the original human inclination to wholesome family living. Theologically, the primary notion which informed the
Puritans' understanding of the marriage relationship was that of
the covenant: "God had established the rules of marriage when
he solemnized the first one, and he had made no changes in
them since then. The covenant of marriage was a promise to
obey those rules without conditions and without reservations."[35]

The Puritans accepted the covenant that God made with
Abraham as also applying to themselves. Just as Abraham responded by promising on behalf of not only himself, but also
his entire family,[36] so it was incumbent upon the Puritan fathers, and by extension mothers, to ensure that all members of
the family, including servants, were good church members and
citizens of the state. Even so, Puritans distinguished between
God's covenant with an individual and various social contracts
of which the family is the primary kind. Although all social covenants originated in God's covenant with the individual, social
covenants had different terms. The covenant of grace (i.e., God's
covenant with the individual) had more to do with the life beyond and required faith, whereas the family, church or state covenant had more to do with the good life in this world and required
obedience expressed in right conduct.[37] Moreover, the enforcement of good behavior on all members of the social covenant
was required to preserve the good fortune of the whole group;

the delinquency of any one member would result in the misfortune of the entire family or community.

Seventeenth-century Puritan preachers also enjoined husbands and wives equally to fulfill a primary responsibility to love each other. One of the chief goods of marriage is that it overcomes the "aloneness of individual existence"; thus, the otherwise highly duty-oriented view of family is explicitly transcended in Puritan descriptions of exemplary husband and wife relationships.

The Puritan writers believed that a chief end of marriage is mutual support and comfort; that sexual and sensual delight is essential to that comfort; that husband and wife must also be the best of friends and that this delight and friendship must last, neither must wane with the years.[38]

Thus, the Puritan theological insight that in the original order of God's creation marriage is good, tempered and informed the covenental ideal with its emphasis on duties and responsibilities that must be enforced against the proclivities of a sinful humanity.

4. Husbands and Wives

Socially and economically, wives of Puritan husbands were significantly better off than most of their contemporaries and historical predecessors. The Puritan preacher, William Gouge, responded to women who apparently objected to his emphasis upon the subordinate status of wives to their husbands by pointing to the mutual duties placed upon husband and wife.[39] The Puritans overcame the biblical injunction of the complete subjection of the wife to the will of the husband by insisting on special duties that husbands held to their wives as well as wives to their husbands. Richard Baxter argued for the conception of "joint property" on the basis that the wife may claim a third of her husband's property in the event of death or divorce.[40] New England laws, strictly enforced, required husbands to make adequate provisions for their spouses on an on-going basis. John Demos has shown that in the Plymouth Colony, the court was willing to award widows more than prescribed in a deceased husband's will if its provisions were deemed inadequate.[41] Griffith advises in his handbook that there are certain households wherein the wife should be given control over the household finances including "where the husband is foolish and weaker and not able to discern what is good for himself and his family."[42] The Puritan wife of New England held an enviable position, even to that of contemporary England, as her husband's authority was legally limited: "He could not lawfully strike her, nor could he command her anything contrary to the laws of God, laws which were explicitly defined in the civil codes."[43]

Matthew Griffith describes the marriage contract, a prerequisite of the Puritan marriages, as a "promise" between two persons to marry each other and an agreement to which the parents of the same have given their consent.[44] In Puritan New England, such intentions to marry had to be announced either at three successive public meetings or by a written notice posted at the town meetinghouse for at least fourteen days.[45] Civil magistrates presided over the wedding ceremony itself only after the obligatory public announcement of marital intentions.[46] Within one month after the ceremony, the bridegroom was required to report the marriage to the town clerk; failure to do so would incur fines. No marriage was considered valid until it was consummated; if the man was impotent, the bride would be freed from the marriage contract. Divorces giving the right to remarry were allowed when either party would prove that the other had neglected basic marital duty. Grounds for such divorce included adultery, desertion, and absence for a length of time to be determined by the civil government. In some colonies, both the husband's failure to provide economic support for his wife and cruelty were possible grounds for divorce. There is ample evidence that the courts often intervened to prevent all of the above-mentioned abuses; punishment for such violations ranged from fines and symbolic executions to public whippings. Puritan society did not tolerate deadbeat dads any more than non-supporting husbands, and fathers who did not adequately provide for their children were fined or given sentences in houses of correction.

It should not be overlooked that the Puritans were a pious people; accordingly, parental responsibility included both the spiritual and the physical well-being of the children. Richard Baxter recommended in his *Christian Directory* that family worship should be followed twice daily and counseled fathers: "You think the calling of ministers honorable and happy, and so it is, because they serve Christ in so high a work; but if you will not neglect it, you may do for your children more than any minister can do."[47]

The Puritans were an eminently practical people as well, and there can be little doubt that the parental obligation was focused on both helping their children to prepare for gainful employment and finding suitable spouses for them. Since many jobs required apprenticeships of seven years to some master of the trade, a child would be sent to live with such a master between the ages of ten and fourteen. Given the age of the child, it is clear that the parents must have had decisive influence in the choice of the children's careers. According to Edmund Morgan, daughters were also apprenticed to other mothers to learn housekeeping. This practice, however, was not unique to Puritanism. The custom of placing children in other families was widely prac-

ticed in England in the seventeenth century and was justified by
Englishmen on the grounds that a child learned better manners
when he was brought up in a home other than his own.

The other primary obligation upon parents was to see that
their children were well married. Again, parental guidance was
most significant and usually two factors were paramount in winning parental consent: religion and wealth. The religious handbooks of the period indicate, unsurprisingly, that ministers urged
that the religious concern should outweigh the economic. Nevertheless, a daughter's parents would be unlikely to offer their
required consent unless they were satisfied that she would be
well taken care of. Likewise, a son's parents would also withhold
consent if the daughter's dowry was deemed insufficient. Puritan parents commonly haggled with zeal over the financial ar-
rangements for their children. The normal ratio was for the girl's
parents to give half as much as the boy's.[48]

Although Puritan parents often suggested a match for their
children, parental guidance was significant but not singularly
decisive. The proposed spouses had to agree to their parents'
recommendations. Again, the religious handbooks clearly limit
parental authority. The rationale for this limitation was that the
common duty of husband and wife was to love each other: "They
must have an intyre (sic) affection to each other."[49] This God-
given duty thus restricted parental authority with respect to their
children's marriage partner; after all, parents could not command
them to that which would violate God's intention that spouses
love one another. While Puritans did not think that the choice
of marriage should be determined by romantic attraction, they
did believe that a devoted and lasting affection between the
spouses should be developed and sustained throughout the marriage. For Puritan poet Ann Bradstreet, perseverance in conjugal
love could even be coupled with salvation in her lyric "To my

Dear and Loving Husband:

> If ever two were one, then surely we.
> If ever man were lov'd by wife, then thee.
> If ever wife was happy in a man,
> Compare with me, ye women, if you can.
> I prize thy love more than whole Mines of gold,
> Or all the riches that the East doth hold.
> My love is such that Rivers cannot quench,
> Nor ought but love from thee give recompence.
> Thy love is such I can no way repay;
> The heavens reward thee manifold I pray.
> Then while we live, in love lets so persever,
> That when we live no more, we may live ever."[50]

5. The Puritan Legacy

In the Puritan worldview, the family is the primary social unit. Both government and church are derivative therefrom, and their raison d'être is to support well-functioning families. Because of the fall, individuals need assistance from the state and church to fulfill their most important responsibilities as husbands and wives as well as parents and children. Thus, weakened and sinful human persons are strengthened by the legal enforcement powers of the state as well as by the spiritual sustenance provided by the church.

According to Puritan theology, the goal of life is the attainment of God-serving families, families wherein human beings enter most fully into spiritual, emotional and physical communion. The attainment of this goal in a sinless world would require the institutions of neither church nor state. Despite the emphasis on economic concerns in Puritan family making and being, Puritans conceived of the family as the original "church" and "state." Within a family, its members would learn all that is needed for rightful participation in the world economically, socially and religiously. The conviction was so strongly held among the Puritans that individuals living outside a family unit were considered anti-social and also detrimental to societal well-being. Thus, in Puritan Massachusetts, selectmen of every town obliged single persons either to set up a household or to join an already existing household, subjecting themselves to the domestic government of its head. The Puritans were a strikingly practical lot who demanded worldly accountability of adults, and whose preachers called upon husbands and wives to be united by bonds of affection subordinated only to the love that each person owed to God.

The heightened expectations for satisfaction within family life, the exaltation of the family as the most valued social institution and a profound ambivalence toward government as both a source for strengthening families and a power potentially disruptive of familial and religious bonds, are enduring contributions of Puritanism to the American national psyche.

THE GREAT AWAKENINGS: THE FEMINIZATION OF RELIGION AND FAMILY

Family historians have long called attention to a change in the nature of the family beginning in the Colonial period and culminating in the nineteenth century wherein the family became increasingly less patriarchal and more affective (warmer); the prevailing metaphor of this family is that of "refuge" from the world.[51] Demos observes that periodization of family types is not precise—the end of one period and start of another often overlap. I would add that older forms persist in instances even when the new is in full bloom. Further, of course, different social classes change at varying rates and times. Although most of these changes began with the gentry, in the eighteenth and nineteenth centuries, it was the middle class that most fervently adopted them and influenced change in classes above and below it. The authoritarian family is gradually displaced by one with measurably greater freedom and stronger affection between husband and wife as well as between parents and children.

Simultaneously, the family becomes increasingly walled-off from the larger community of kin and wider society, enhancing the dependence and expectations of nuclear family members upon each other. This intensification of feelings within the family was most pronounced in both Britain and the United States and cannot be adequately explained by economic and political changes. Indeed, such economic and political changes may be heavily dependent on prior changes in the family.[52]

Again, we shall see that religion played a central role in the transformation of family life in the eighteenth and nineteenth centuries. As already indicated, the seventeenth-century Puritan emphasis on the importance of spousal love as an internal dimension of "holy matrimony" had an unintended contrary consequence of limiting parental authority over their children's mate selection. More importantly, the focus on the individual's spiritual life and conscience, which required valuing the interior life, was critical to the upgrading of affect in familial relationships.

Like his spiritual forebears, the Puritans, the central figure of the first Great Awakening, Jonathan Edwards, is most unlikely to evoke images of excessive emotion. Yet his own contemporary critics, most often envious fellow clergymen, accused Edwards of filling the church with confusion by whipping people into emotional frenzies.[53] Edwards responded to the accusation by stating his conviction that the human emotions or affections were not in conflict with human reason and will because they were all derived from the one God. Before his own marriage, Edwards recorded his attraction to his future bride, describing her as singing while being full of joy and pleasure; even when alone in fields she is enjoying "an invisible presence conversing with her."[54] In all likelihood, Edward's estimation of his future bride's special relationship to the divine and her overall attractiveness were inseparable.

Beyond Edwards, other Great Awakening preachers demanded that believers respond to Christ in heart; George Whitefield, a revivalist of the Awakening, chastised ministers for "preaching an unknown and unfelt Christ."[55] The new Christianity of the Great Awakenings (especially the second) is thus a religion of the heart. As we will see, the second Awakening was to become a vehicle for raising women to the head of the family.

The Second Great Awakening, beginning around 1800, proclaimed Christianity even more emphatically as a religion of the heart, not the head, "just as it had become a religion chiefly of women rather than men."[56] From the beginning of the nineteenth century, their congregations comprised predominantly of women, New England ministers preached that mothers were more important than fathers in the raising and educating of children. This emphasis was, of course, a departure from earlier views that entrusted only the physical well-being of children to mothers and left moral, religious and intellectual formation to fathers. Converging with changes in the economy, as production moved out of the home and to a system of owners and workers defined by wages and prices, Christianity's new focus on women is responsible for the appearance of the reign of domesticity. Accordingly, the domains of the world (business and public life) and of the home were divided, seemingly hermetically sealed, the one to be ruled by men and the other by women.

Further, Christianity gave diametrically contrary assessments of the spiritual and moral value of the two realms, effectively equating the home with heaven and the world with sin.[57] In so doing, women, who for most of Western history were considered less spiritual and more earthly while men were deemed the morally superior, became the protector and transmitter of religious values. Still barred from virtually all other public roles and associations, women now began to join voluntary associations which were almost all religiously inspired. The various morality-oriented movements of the nineteenth century, such as The Boston Female Moral Reform Society, specifically opposed the double standard of sexual morality. Nancy Cott has described the ideology of these organizations as encouraging women's self-esteem and denying "female inferiority outright," while disapproving of women's subservience to men's whims and wishes."[58] To be sure, one motive for the emphasis on companionate bonds between husband and wife in marriage was the diminishment of adultery in society and the confining of passion to the marriage bed.

The elevation of the spiritual status of women must be seen as a critical element in establishing an ethos of more egalitarian spousal relationships. Indeed, Christianity's role in elevating the status of women was repeatedly used by ministers and others to coax women to devote themselves to religious associations and activities. In his sermon before the members of The Boston Female Asylum, Joseph Buchminister asserted that women's devotion to religion was their recompense for the Gospel's service in making "men willing to treat females as equals, and in some respect, as superiors" and "only Christianity redeemed human nature from the base passions and taught reverence for domestic relations."[59]

Many female charitable organizations responded generously to requests to support missionary activities abroad, apparently because they found appeals on behalf of women persuasive. The trustees of the New Hampshire Mission Society, for example, described women in other lands as "never treated by the other sex as companions and equals. They are in great measure outcasts from society. They are made to minister to the pleasures of man; they are made to do the work of men; but admitted to the enjoyment of equal rights, and raised to the respectability and happiness of free and honourable social intercourse, they are not." The authority and respect which women enjoyed at home in Christian America enhanced, in their eyes, the credibility of the Church's claims to be able to improve the plight of women overseas.

By the end of the nineteenth century, Christianity had succeeded in offering a distinct sphere of both authority and responsibility to women, namely the home. From the point of view of the internal dynamics of the family, and most especially the husband-wife relationship, an extraordinary revolution had taken place.

CONCLUSION: THE SHRINKING ROLES OF HUSBANDS AND FATHERS

In his brilliant study, *Families Against the City*, sociologist Richard Sennett demonstrates the profound transformation of family life occurring in the Union Park neighborhood of Chicago during the last third of the nineteenth century.[60] In so doing, he provides a description of the changes in family life pertaining more broadly to the nation and persisting in some respects into the early twenty-first century. The older aristocratic families of Union Park from before the Civil War had been led unequivocally by their fathers, whose prominence outside the family, especially in the church, was the source of authority and respect within the house: "...his leadership in the church was a sign of his own virtue and his family were expected to obey him, since it was he who voiced and embodied the laws of religion."[61] Al-

though austerely moral, these families were by no means iso-
lated, but enjoyed an active and extensive social life.[62] Indeed,
in addition to the church, the aristocratic families maintained a
diversity of primary group affiliations.

In the period from 1872-1890, however, Union Park became
a predominantly middle-class neighborhood, whose families dif-
fered greatly not only from their immediate upper-class predecessors, but also from families of modest means in previous eras.
In the new families of Union Park, the wives, rather than the
husbands, were the authority figures.[63] Sennett notes the "striking feature" of docile husbands withdrawing from social life outside the home, which becomes the only focus outside of work
for human contact. Sennett perceptively observes that the shift
in authority between men and women in the family is mirrored
in the change of patterns of participation outside the home: "The
men were no longer the church leaders, for example; this activity had been taken over by the women."[64] The resulting feminization and intensification of family life led to children feeling
that the father did not really matter much at all.

The story of the changing relationship between parents and
children is the concern of the next chapter. It is important to
note, however, that a veritable reversal of roles within the family
was accomplished by virtue of the radically altered view of the
moral authority of women and men, which in large part was the
effect of developments in American Christianity.[65] Given the
imbalance in the relative authority and spiritual estimation of
men/husbands and women/wives throughout history, the influence of Christianity becomes all the more significant. It is doubt-
ful that true equality between husband and wife could ever be
achieved without such a period of radical reassessment of the
husband-wife relationship occurring first in the spiritual dimension of life.

3

And What of the Children?: Religion and the Status of the Child in Western Society

In June 1997, an 18-year-old woman delivered her infant son in a bathroom stall during her senior prom. After cutting the umbilical cord, she choked him and put him in a plastic bag that she knotted and then threw away. She hurriedly returned to her prom date, danced and ate a salad.[1] On March 17, 1992, two-and-a-half year-old Saonnia Bolder was beaten and scalded to death by Sadie Williams, her mother. The mother, angered because her young daughter had wet herself, laid the child in the bathtub and poured scalding water over her genitals and buttocks. The autopsy on Saonnia's body revealed sixty-two cuts, bruises, burns, abrasions and wrist scars, among other injuries; eleven were still healing.[2]

Psychopathetic mistreatment of children is not unique to late twentieth century America. The ritualized sacrifice of children in ancient Semitic civilizations was sanctioned, and the killing of children in the Greco-Roman world was legal. Still, in our supposedly enlightened modern age, there are indicators which produce consternation, not the least of which is the previously discussed increase of out-of-wedlock teenage mothers and single parents.[3]

It is not hard to imagine that future students of the history of the child will characterize the present period as both "the worst of times and the best of times." We live in a time of heightened confusion with a marked ambivalence toward children. Today, the full spectrum of parent-child relationships, from the most abusive and hurtful to the most humane and caring (each dominant, as we will show, in different historical periods) are dramatically juxtaposed.

While the status of the child is thus ambiguous in contemporary society, it is also true, as suggested above, that the place of the child in society is much more secure now than in civilizations past. From the long view of history, there is again overwhelming evidence that Christianity has played a central role in the elevation of the status of children from infancy through adolescence in the West, and that the residual impact has undoubtedly been global in scope. (In speaking of the status of children, I refer to the dominant social standards of valuing children, of valuing the nurturing of their personal potential, and of the respect given their life and death.) Just as Christianity has been of the greatest significance in affirming life-long monogamous marriage as the Western marital norm, so it has played a leading role in establishing the appreciation of childhood as a sacred time of life and in establishing children as having absolute value, equal to that of adult human beings. As with the Western marital norm, the Christian normative view of the value of children was secured only after a fierce battle with opposing views, reflecting diminished estimations of children.

EARLY CHRISTIANITY OPPOSES INFANTICIDE
AND CHILD ABANDONMENT

John Sommerville concluded in his study, *The Rise and Fall of Childhood*, that "...the beginning of the Christian era marks a revolution in the child's status."[4] Just as the founding fathers of even modern nation states have profound impact on the nations to which they give birth, the foundational figures of religion shape their historical communities by their recorded words and deeds. Indeed, this shaping may be even more powerful and enduring because of the transcendent authority with which founders of religions are believed by their devotees to be endued. Thus, we are not surprised once again to find that Jesus is the most radical and effective exponent of the revolution in the child's status. In an extraordinary transvaluation of values, Jesus exalted the child and the child-like state: "People were bringing little children to him, for him to touch them. The disciples turned them away, but when Jesus saw this he was indignant and said to them, 'Let the little children come to me; do not stop them; for it is to such as these that the Kingdom of God belongs. I tell you solemnly, anyone who does not welcome the Kingdom of God like a little child will never enter it.' Then he put his arms around them, laid his hands on them and gave them his blessing." (Mark 10:13-16; Matthew 19:13-15; Luke 18:15-17) Important here is not only Jesus' solicitude for children over against his own disciples' apparent indifference, but also his affirmation that childhood is an essentially good state qualifying one for the Kingdom of Heaven. Also important is that here, and in all other of his references to children, Jesus is not dealing with exceptional cases. For Jesus, even the typical child is noteworthy.

While the New Testament repeats the commandment of the Hebrew Bible that children honor their parents, it avers that parents also have obligations to their children. Ephesians 6:4 warns parents to "never drive your children to resentment." The New Testament also affirms that parents are expected to provide for their children and not children for their parents (II Corinthians 12:14b); while perhaps this statement appears to the modern mind as totally obvious, it has nevertheless been honored in the breach for children in most of Western history. Jesus' words on the value of children, the moral equivalent of his teaching on marriage as enjoining life-long, mutual, monogamous commitment, would take even longer than the latter to become the norm for Western civilization and to inform the thought and practice of its predominant child-rearing tradition.

As already mentioned, both infanticide and the abandonment of infants by their mothers occur in contemporary America. However, these are hardly common events and are considered barbarous. They are also illegal. The abandonment of children in the ancient world, however, was neither illegal nor considered barbarous. John Boswell estimated that twenty to forty percent of urban children were abandoned by their natal parents in Rome during the first three centuries.[5] Moreover, exposure (leaving a child in a public place) was not illegal; the state did not prohibit nor punish parents for abandoning their children, and there was no effective ecclesiastical judicial system to impose the pain of excommunication.[6] The fact that Roman law allowed a natal parent to retrieve an exposed child without punishment so long as he reimbursed the guardians' maintenance expenses, demonstrates that the act of abandonment was fundamentally acceptable.[7] Indeed, given the near absolute power of the Roman father over the life and death of members of his household (including wife, lineal descendants and slaves), child abandonment must have been difficult to critique from within Roman culture.

Through the time of Virgil society recognized the right of a father to kill even a grown son.[8] Actually, since infanticide was legal and practiced, abandonment must have often been seen as a merciful alternative.

Until the fourth century, in both Rome and Greece infanticide was not objected to by either the law or public opinion. Beginning with the reign of the first Christian Emperor Constantine, however, the legal system began to discourage infanticide:

> A law should be written on bronze or waxed tablets or on linen cloth, and posted throughout all the municipalities of Italy, to restrain the hands of parents from infanticide and turn their hopes to birth.... If any parent should repent that he had offspring which on account of poverty he is unable to rear, there shall be no delay in issuing food and clothing since the rearing of a newborn infant can not tolerate delay..."[9]

Comparing later European sources, Hugh Cunningham has characterized the Roman and Greek sources as evincing "a relative neglect of younger children."[10] He points out that when discussed, children are seen in terms of their deficiencies, "the adult qualities which they lack."[11] In classical Athens, children were seen as "physically weak, morally incompetent and mentally incapable."[12] Cicero considered that "childhood itself could not be praised but only its potential."[13]

As we shall see shortly, Christianity elevated the status of children to that of being equal to adults in the eyes of God. All human beings, from infants to adults, have absolute value as a result of their relationship to God and their sempiternal nature— once born they will live forever. Acting on such belief (inherited from Judaism), and in contrast to the Greeks and Romans, Christians declared that infanticide was murder. In 374, the Christian emperors Valentinian, Valens and Gratian decreed that "If anyone, man or woman, should commit the sin of killing any infant, that crime should be punishable with death."[14] Cunningham suggests that the law was originally directed at pagan ritual killing of children, but later was interpreted as a blanket condemnation of infanticide. The distance between this law and the Roman law code of twelve tables (fifth century B.C.) requiring that any child deformed at birth be put to death, is considerable. While outlawing infanticide, however, the Christian emperors did not elect to outlaw the abandonment of children; rather church and state in the fourth century conspired to regulate the practice and decrease the worst instances of abuse.

Fundamental to the difference in the Church's response to abandonment as distinguished from infanticide was its awareness that parents abandoned children most often because they did not want to see their children killed. The Christian writer Lactanius (c. 240-320) explicitly acknowledges that "parents expose children when they do *not* wish to kill them."[15] Notwithstanding this distinction, Lactanius, as well as almost all Christian writers from the mid-second century through the early fourth century, disapproved strongly of child abandonment.[16] Some Christian writers considered abandonment to be the equivalent of murder. This view was expressed by Athenagoras (*Legatio Pro Christianis* 35) and also Clement of Alexandria. Clement in fact described those who would abandon their children as "child killers" (*Stromateis* 2:18).

As suggested above, this posture contrasts strongly with Classical and Hellenistic philosophers who did not object to abandonment; both Plato and Aristotle, for example, accepted abandonment without reservation.[17] Also, only two philosophers actually writing at Rome, Epictetus and Musonius Rufus, both Stoics, objected to abandonment. John Boswell's assessment here is decisive: "Most ancient moral writers evince indifference toward or acceptance of abandonment."[18] Thus, the Christian writers' reaction to the abandonment of children in the Roman Empire is all the more impressive.

Christian reflection on abandonment was to develop and embrace a more nuanced understanding of the diverse motivations and circumstances leading to its too prevalent practice. Most early Christian writers were from the upper class of society. Their common accusation that child abandonment was an "indulgence of the wealthy, exclusively for convenience"[19] confirms that the upper classes also exposed children. Undoubtedly the motivation of the wealthy was quite different from the disenfranchised and poorer classes, who felt compelled by adversity to abandon their children. It would take some time longer, however, for Christian moral reflection to represent adequately the predicament of the latter in its moral discourse.

Why did the rich abandon their children? It may be that the wealthy had greater interest in seeing their abandoned children killed, as Roman law permitted foundlings to recover their free status and inheritance rights. One motive for the abandonment of children by wealthy fathers may have been to keep family estates intact. However, given the rights of the Roman father (*paterfamilias*), it is hard to imagine that such concerns could not have been satisfied, regardless of the number of descendants. Thus, convenience seems to be a rather fair estimation of motivation among the wealthy. Further, some ideal number of children for a family may have been operative; few sources point to a Roman family with many children.[20]

Given the absence of effective contraceptive devices, it is likely that the overwhelming majority of Roman families directly participated in the abandonment of children. Abandonment in the Roman world was of three general kinds: (1) exposure; (2) outright sale of a child; and (3) substitution (wherein a barren woman pretended to have given birth to the child given or sold to her by the abandoning parents). The upper classes probably restricted themselves to the first kind of abandonment: exposing the child in a public place. Although the poorer classes also availed themselves of this method, which was the most common of the three, they would also utilize the other two options of sale and substitution. While children sold or exposed would most likely become slaves, the substituted child had the greatest chance to be accepted as a beloved child, as he/she was to be known as a lineal descendant of the father. Hence, there sometimes emerged elaborate plans of deception to lead neighbors and relatives to believe the foster mother gave birth to the child.

Even the most optimistic assessments of the fate of abandoned children[21] do not disallow the "considerable extent" to which such children were used as slaves and prostitutes.[22] Apparently, the demand for child prostitutes was sufficient to trigger popular fears about the theft of children for that purpose.[23] As Beverly Rawson has noted, two emperors within a fifty-year span of time legislated to prohibit the castration of slave boys; child eunuchs were highly preferred sex objects of older men.[24] Christian writers, beginning with Justin Martyr (*I Apology* 27) and a long line of successors, decried the widespread use of abandoned children as prostitutes.

By the fourth century, Christian reflection on abandonment would consider fully the direct consequences for the children involved but would also recognize the differing motives of parents. St. Basil of Caeserea (c. 330-79) describes three categories of parents who abandon their children, ascribing to each a different moral status. First there is the mother who, motivated by ill-will toward the child or the desire to conceal her own sin, despises her child and abandons it to certain death on a deserted road. She should be given the maximum penalty. Second, Basil deals with the middle-class whom he suspects of inordinate concern with inheritance: "This is like those parents who expose their infants pleading poverty; or even make unequal distribution among their children in arranging their estates. It would be just, since they have given each equally a share of life, also to give each equally and uniformly a share in the means of living."[25] Basil reveals here his Christian sentiments that all children deserve equal opportunity for a prosperous life. Third, Basil turns his attention to the desperate situation of the urban poor. He describes with great poignancy the father "conquered by necessity and inexorable need" to sell one of his children:

> Then what are his thoughts? Which one shall I sell first? Which one will the grain auctioneer favor the most? Should I start with the oldest? But I am reluctant to do so because of his age. The youngest? I pity his youth and inexperience of life. That one is the spitting image of his parents. This one is so quick to learn. What horrible misery! What is to become of me? Which one of them shall I afflict? What sort of animal am I turning into? How can I ignore my natural feelings? If I hold on to them all I will see all of them die of hunger, but if I sell one, how will I face the rest having become the suspect of treachery in their eyes? How will I live in a household which I myself have deprived of a child? How will I come to the table when its contents were obtained in this way?[26]

How far we have come from the insouciance of the classical and Hellenistic pagan authors who have treated the same subject!

St. Basil further directs his moral indignation against the auctioneer who handles the sale of children brought to his block by parents coerced by poverty: "after a thousand tears (the father) comes to sell a beloved child, but no pity moves you; you do not defer to value. Hunger has made him desperate; you delay and dissemble, prolonging his agony. He asks for the price of food in return for his own heart, but you—not only does your hand not shrink from wringing profit from his misery, but you dicker with him for more, bargaining eagerly to get a better deal, piling further suffering on the desperate." Through such writings, St. Basil of Caeserea came to play the central role in shaping the theological and institutional response of the Eastern Church to children, especially the disadvantaged. In addition to his writings, Basil established hospitals and hostels for the poor who were cared for through the system of relief which he conceived.

In the West, Christian emperors and Roman bishops cooperated to protect children. They also evinced considerable sympathy for impoverished parents while chastising the well-to-do who abandoned or neglected their children. Valentinian II, in 391, allowed parents to reclaim children sold into slavery without requiring them to repay those who had reared them:

> All those whom the pitiful circumstances of their parents, lacking sustenance, have relegated to slavery should be restored to their original free status. Nor may any repayment be demanded, since the service of a free person for a considerable length of time should suffice.[27]

Some sixty years later, in 451, the Western Emperor Valentinian III amended the prevailing law and insisted that "buyers be reimbursed at a rate of twenty percent above what they paid."[28] For Valentinian III, it was important, under the worsening circumstances of the Western empire, not to discourage buyers who may offer the only hope of survival for some children, but at the same time it was important to preserve the opportunity for the children to regain their liberty:

> So that neither will the buyer—who gets back more than he paid on the price—be sorry to have bought (the child) under such wretched and desperate circumstances, nor will freedom succumb to the weight of misfortune.

Church leaders did not agree with this perspective, however

much they would like to see a greater generosity prevail. St. Ambrose, Bishop of Milan from 374 to 397, continued to castigate the rich as child-killers for failing to nurse their children and for abandoning some so to increase the inheritance of others.[29] Ambrose does not find parents forced by adverse circumstances to sell their children to be morally culpable; rather, he condemns the wealthy who either exploit the situation or refuse to help.[30] It was, as Boswell rightly notes, the church and not the state that had "more effect on both thought and behavior regarding most family issues."[31] Theodosius made bishops the arbiters in several family matters, and when he threatened to consign parents to the mines who forced their daughters into prostitution, he directed that girls abused in this way appeal to the Bishop, not to a civil authority.[32] Increasingly, the religious leaders of the early church concern themselves with ensuring that children are properly cared for.[33]

While the church was devoted to working with the results of parents who brought into the world children they were unable to care for, it persisted in focusing on the cause of the suffering. In the absence of effective contraceptive devices, intercourse between men and women in their childbearing years often produced offspring. Thus, Augustine and earlier Christian writers elevated the procreative purpose as the central and even the exclusive justification of sexuality. By focusing on the procreative function of sexuality, Christians sought not only to rationalize the sexual act, but also to attend to the direct cause of unwanted and uncared for children in the ancient world. Here are to be found the theological roots of contemporary Christian-inspired abstinence-based teen pregnancy and sexual disease (including AIDS prevention) programs. Christian educators in the ancient world sought to bring to full consciousness the consequences of sexual intercourse which, as we have discussed, included infanticide and, more commonly, abandonment with the possibilities of the most demeaning abuses. The church understood the failure to behave responsibly in sexual matters, including the taking of full responsibility for the children born from sexual intimacy, to be a betrayal of both divine and human love.

How much can we infer from the widespread abandonment of children about the quality of parent-child relationships in the ancient world? Even the most severe critic of the past of the parental abuse of children, Lloyd de Mause (author of the oft-quoted statement: " the history of childhood is a nightmare from which we have only recently begun to awaken."[34]), allowed that parents of the past had tender feelings and loved their children.[35] It would be unfair to conclude that parents who abandoned their children were abusive and uncaring towards them, or that they were uncaring towards their remaining children. Few today would accuse those having abortions or approving of them (perhaps the majority), of being therefore necessarily uncaring parents to those children which they choose to rear. The more significant issue is to determine the ideological and social conditions shaping parent-child relationships. In this regard, the *patria potestas*, the near absolute power of fathers over the members of their household, must be understood as a decisive factor. In accordance with this principle, children's obligations to their parents and to the state were emphasized, but duties running in the other direction were not. Accordingly, mention of parental obligations to children and the welfare of children is relatively rare in other than Christian sources: "the overriding impression derived from the ancient sources is that childhood was not seen as important for itself...Moreover, it was common to consider children, not as individual human beings, but in terms of the services they could render their parents, partly in continuing the line, but also as supports in old age, and in carrying out essential rituals at the time of the parents' death."[36] As mentioned previously (see Chapter One), Augustus legislated that women produce children, but his intention was to increase the numbers of the privileged classes as well as to assure the state necessary manpower; it was not to promote the love of children.[37] Thus, we are compelled to correlate the new emphasis on the care and love of children which becomes manifest with the emergence of Christianity.

MEDIEVAL CHRISTIAN IMAGES OF THE CHILD: A TRUST FROM GOD

At the start and towards the end of the Middle Ages (the late fifth and sixth centuries, as well as the fourteenth and fifteenth centuries), Europe, as a result of war, calamities and the plagues, twice experienced death on a massive scale, reducing its entire population by half. Under such circumstances, the Christian concern for existence in an after-life was persistently and immediately compelling for the overwhelming majority of medieval fathers, mothers, children, brothers and sisters. St. Augustine, a pivotal figure, who both culminates the ancient period of Christianity and initiates medieval Catholicism, describes in detail the apparently solipsistic behavior of infants, offering it as evidence of a fallen nature inherited from the sinful parents of humankind, Adam and Eve.[38] Augustine's emphasis on infant depravity served as a belated theological explanation of infant baptism, an earlier and widespread practice of Christians. More importantly, it paradoxically elevated the importance of the moral status of children. As Hugh Cunningham rightly remarked:

"Augustine's view of original sin put the child as a human being on a par with an adult, not incomplete, and that its moral dilemmas needed to be taken as seriously as if it were six feet tall."[39] The failure of parents to have their infants baptized as early as possible was considered a grievous sin, as it compounded the common tragedy of an early death with eternal damnation for the deceased.[40]

Shulamith Shahar has noted how the negative image of Augustine, who nevertheless understood the baptized child to be "more innocent than his elders," merged with a more explicitly positive image of the child in medieval Christianity.[41] Medieval views inclining to a positive image of children hearkened to Jesus' words in Matthew 18: "become as little children." For medieval scholars, childhood was conceived of as "the period of purity, innocence and faith and the equivalence between children and angels was established."[42] Anticipating themes of nineteenth-century Romanticism, childhood was seen as a period of innocence, with adulthood symbolizing the loss of innocence. Even the child's prayers were seen as stronger and more efficacious, which perception gave rise to the practice of the youngest child of the family offering grace before meals. Boswell observed that Christians were more emphatic about the call to "loving parenthood" than others: "children were idealized and parental attachment to them assumed."[43] Shahar contrasts favorably the medieval view of child-rearing, encouraging tenderness up to the age of seven, to that of the Enlightenment, which endorsed rigid discipline from the earliest age. In medieval society, a stricter disciplinary approach was generally followed for children from the age of seven with controlled whipping being widely endorsed and no doubt practiced.[44] Thomas Aquinas theologized that the suffering caused by such beating was one of the manifestations of the punishment imposed on humans as a consequence of Original Sin. However, as early as the eleventh century, Anselm of Canterbury opposed beating in monasteries as an improper disciplinary measure and instead advocated for "tolerant, non-violent education, by means of personal example, compassion, love, encouragement and correction when necessary."[45] In any case, it seems that whipping was reserved for boys; girls were generally exempted from such discipline.[46]

Medieval Christian culture transformed the dominant Roman view of the parent-child relationship, that of the Roman *patria potestas* which understood children as property of the father, who had the right to determine whether they were to live or die, into one in which children were considered to be " a trust from God."[47] To do this, Christianity used its vast organization of religious instructors and parish preachers to disseminate its message of parental responsibility for children. Perhaps even more effective, was the repeated iconographic representation of the Holy Family as an ideal type to be imitated by all Christian families: thus in the twelfth century, Mary, variously depicted as pregnant, suckling her son and playing with or caressing him, became for all the example of the devoted mother.[48] Similarly, in the fourteenth and fifteenth centuries, Joseph was represented as the archetypal ideal father, protector of Mary and the infant Jesus. The worship of the infant Jesus flourished in the twelfth century; in the thirteenth century, the manger was introduced into churches and thereafter Christmas became a family-centered feast in which special concern was expressed for children.

Medieval Christianity developed two traditions that had a major impact on the quality of life for children: oblation (the offering of children for service to God) and godparents. Catholic reservations concerning kin relationships led to the institution of supplemental parents, called godparents, who pledged to fulfill the duties of educating their godchildren about the Christian faith.[49] The godparents, who could be anyone—friend, patron or relative (other than the biological parents)—represented a new relationship which focused on children's spiritual well-being; this relationship also led to material support in some instances. godparenting enhanced "the position of affective kinship in Christian culture."[50] Despite all this, Christianity in the Middle Ages could not arrest the abandonment of children by their parents.

In any event, the church, because of its concern for children, changed the typical place where children were abandoned from the road to the church doorsteps; thereafter, Christianity introduced oblation or the donation of a child as a permanent "gift" to a monastery.[51] Boswell has described oblation as "dramatically altering the terms of servitude" affecting abandoned children in the West.[52] Indeed, by the early seventh century, the practice of offering children to religious service had already become firmly entrenched, and many wealthy parents who would have abandoned their children on the road came to entrust them to a protected environment where they were assured children were properly fed and clothed. Given the dominant medieval values, the child "abandoned" to a monastery, instead of possibly suffering the fate of a slave, prostitute or other social outcast, would now enjoy the special social status which religious life conferred in the medieval world. This status might also afford significant influence in the secular world, as clerical leaders exercised political, economic and cultural authority in medieval society. Parents of oblates received nothing in return and often made substantial contributions to the monastery for accepting their children. For poorer children, service in the church offered the possibility of a successful and important career despite humble origins.[53]

After two centuries of progress, relative prosperity and decreases in child abandonment, the thirteenth and fourteenth centuries, ravaged by natural and man-made disasters, witnessed a return to high rates of abandonment. Again, parish churches came to be the primary institution to care for such abandoned children. During this period, foundling hospitals were opened by the church and accommodated a small number of children. Unfortunately, this number was to increase in subsequent centuries despite appalling mortality rates, primarily the consequence of communicable disease and the medical ignorance of the age.[54] The Church was considerably more effective in its campaign opposing both infanticide and the "accidental overlaying" of children; this practice, involving the suffocation of children laying in their parents' bed, appears to have been widely known as one way parents rid themselves of unwanted infants.[55] In the ninth century, the church pronounced prohibitions against the taking of infants into the parental bed.[56] In the eleventh and twelfth centuries, the church heightened its opposition to these practices and acknowledged that both "carelessness as well as evil intent" on the part of parents played a role in infant deaths.[57] Thirteenth-century English synodal legislation identified both the deliberate killing of infants as well as negligent overlaying as major sins, punishment for which should be adjudicated by the Bishop. Furthermore, in every diocese, English priests were ordered to instruct women in their parishes concerning their responsibility to safeguard the lives of their children.[58] By the end of the Middle Ages, the cumulative efforts of the church on behalf of its younger members could not entirely eliminate the harshness of life for children; it did, however, raise societal expectations of greater parental care.

CONFLICTING CHILD-REARING TRADITIONS IN THE SIXTEENTH THROUGH EIGHTEENTH CENTURIES: CHRISTIAN VS. SECULAR MODELS

In 1524, Martin Luther wrote the mayors and aldermen of the cities of Germany imploring them to support elementary education for as many children as possible.[59] Luther explained that even if there were not sound religious reasons for compulsory universal education (which he certainly felt there to be), there were sufficient civil rationales for it: "Even if there were no soul (as I have already said) and men did not need schools and the languages for the sake of Christianity and the Scriptures, still for the establishment of the best schools everywhere, both for boys and girls, this consideration is of itself sufficient, namely that society for the maintenance of civil order and the proper regulation of the household, needs accomplished and well-trained men and women."[60] He believed that children had a God-given inclination to learn which would make flogging in most instances unnecessary and indeed counterproductive.[61] (I will return to the issue of corporal punishment shortly.) While it would take nearly three and one-half centuries before Luther's ideal of universal state-sponsored education would be actualized in the West, Protestants, like Catholics before them, would found new schools and make charitable donations to enable access to education. Further, Protestantism articulated both the spiritual and secular rationale for such education that would have a profound impact on children's lives.

Protestants effected more immediately the spiritualization of the household.[62] Believing that the family was the training ground for successful participation in all other social organizations, including the church and the state, Protestants promoted a new focus on the family. Prayers and Bible readings became part of the daily routine of the family. As has been widely noted, the role and authority of the father of the family was augmented, perhaps in part as a reaction to the displacement, in Protestantism, of the Catholic priest or "father." Already with the religious humanism of Erasmus, the father's responsibility to educate his children, especially the males, was greatly emphasized; with the rise of Protestantism, however, the father assumed an additional role, that of spiritual leadership. It was he who was to read Scripture and offer prayer. Whereas, in Catholicism infant baptism assured the salvation of children, the committed Protestant parents aspired to awaken in their children an awareness of the necessity of salvation. Protestants printed large numbers of catechisms which were used in question-and-answer sessions between parents and children.[63] The ideal Protestant home became a micro-church, wherein parents, most especially the father, stood as minister before their congregant children. In both Protestant and Counter-Reformation Catholic literature, the sacred as well as secular duties of parents towards their children were greatly emphasized.

Puritan authors such as Robert Cleaver and William Gouge elaborated at length on the duties parents hold to their children. Gouge also explains that the source and motive of parental responsibility is love and that God planted love in the hearts of parents so they could gladly bear the "paine, cost and care" on behalf of their children.[64] Only after expounding for fifty pages on such duties does Gouge briefly address the issue of discipline, where he mentions spanking as a last resort. Moreover Gouge, like other Puritan authors, laid down several conditions before a parent should exercise this last resort, including determining that the child actually committed the wrong in question. Further, the parent was never to spank his children to vent his own anger, but only to change the child's behavior. In the end, Gouge advises that it is better to err on the side of leniency because the opposite extreme of severity violates the previously described essence of parenting.

Other Puritans such as Cotton Mather explicitly spoke out against physical punishment. Linda A. Pollock, in her groundbreaking study, *Forgotten Children*, has demonstrated from a broad study of primary sources that Puritan parents did not practice a parenting policy of "breaking the will of the child" as some modern scholarship has proposed.[65] Indeed, Pollock finds "inexplicable" some historians' claim that sixteenth- and seventeenth-century parents were "unmoved" at the loss of a child.[66] Martin Luther's own expression of grief at the loss of two of his six children is instructive. He describes his emotional response to the death of his eight-month-old daughter, Elizabeth: "exquisitely sick, my heart rendered soft and weak. Never had I thought that a father's heart could be so broken for his children's sake." When an older daughter, Magdalene, dies at thirteen, Luther expresses the grief felt by both him and his wife, despite believing in her salvation: "the force of our natural love is so great that we are unable to do this without crying and grieving in our hearts...the features, the words, and the movement of our living and dying daughter, who was so very obedient and respectful, remain engraved in our hearts; even the death of Christ...is unable to take all this away as it should."[67]

It was, in fact, not Protestantism but Enlightenment ideology which was to impose a harsher, relentlessly rational approach to Western child-rearing. John Locke's *Some Thoughts Concerning Education* (1763), repeatedly published in English as well as French, German, Italian, Dutch and Swedish editions, came to have a powerful influence on western parents throughout the eighteenth century. Whereas Catholic and Protestant Reformers were concerned with the education of all children, including the poorest of the society, Locke was admittedly primarily concerned with the upbringing of the well-to-do, specifically addressing the roles that upper-class boys would assume in society.[68] Locke's work, however, assured him a place as guide for "innumerable middle-class families" of the eighteenth and early nineteenth centuries.[69]

According to Pollock, beginning with eighteenth-century British diaries and continuing into the nineteenth and early twentieth centuries, parents evince the belief that the "child could be molded into shape."[70] These texts show parents' concern with having their children comply with the parents' will, molding the character of children, and breaking the child's will. Pollock wonders rightly whether the children would agree with the historians' consensus view that the eighteenth century was really more humane than previous periods.[71]

Locke's influence on such diarists is apparent; in some he is explicitly referenced as their authority.[72] Locke discouraged parents from "coddling" children and recommended that they be bathed in cold water and be made to play outside in harsh weather.[73] His suggestions for enhancing the productivity of destitute children offered the cloak of respectability to barbaric treatment in the industrial revolution (see next page).

The Enlightenment ideal for children's education and rearing was the production of model citizens. This thought reached an apogee in the French Revolution with Danton's assertion that children belong to society more than to their families, and Robespierre's claim that the country should raise children who should be shielded from the prejudices of individual parents.[74]

Herein lies a critical point of difference between religiously oriented perspectives of child rearing and humanistic approaches. The former posit a transcendent ideal, such as salvation, allowing for deviance from social norms. An example is the Puritan provision that children should disobey a parent when in conflict with the will of God; a social space for individual conscience is thus an inherent possibility. In contrast, the Enlightenment ideal of raising socially acceptable children is, contrary to popular belief, more liable to result in oppressive child-rearing practices centered on self-referential social norms in which there is limited opportunity for internal criticism.

In a similar vein, the religious Reformation and its successor traditions were more prone than the Renaissance, and certainly the Enlightenment to accept and apply universal standards of education and child rearing. One motivation for such approaches lay in the Reformation commitment to nurture a Christian who was morally and spiritually worthy of eternal heavenly reward— a possibility which was regarded as being open to all individuals (or at least the excluded are not known in this world). In comparison, humanism and the Enlightenment focused on raising an elite who were to assume leadership of the earthly realm.

The common sense and utilitarian perspective toward children championed by enlightenment thinkers was to contribute to the emergence of a culture that allowed a new level of economic exploitation of youth, particularly those of the less fortunate. John Locke espoused the view that poor children should be put to work by the age of three, with a "bellyful of bread daily to be supplemented by, in winter, if it be thought needful, a little warm water gruel."[75] In England, by the second half of the eighteenth century, poor children were put to work in "Houses of Industry."[76] The new conditions created by the Industrial

Revolution greatly enhanced the economic profitability of exploiting child labor. As we shall see, in both Britain and especially the United States, Christians were to lead the movement for child labor reform.[77]

THE SENTIMENTALIZATION OF CHILDREN: NINETEENTH- AND TWENTIETH-CENTURY CHRISTIANITY

The Christian belief in transcendence and eternity was the source of its challenge in America to a purely this-worldly, instrumentalist view of children. This challenge was most effectively raised by Christian evangelists starting from Jonathan Edwards and by successive periodic eruptions of intensive, affective religiosity. Organized reform efforts, both of Christian clergy and, most especially, of Christian women, also played a decisive role.

Jonathan Edwards himself was particularly impressed with the religious experiences of children. We have already mentioned his description of thirteen-year-old Sarah Pierpont, four years before his marriage to her. In his 1742 *Some Thoughts Concerning the Revival*, Edwards, without attribution, makes note of Sarah's spiritual experiences, defining them as "transporting views and rapturous affections" which are accompanied by two sentiments: an abhorrence towards judging others, wishing instead that the other experienced the love of God more deeply than oneself; and a heightened sense of "the importance of moral social duties, and how great a part of religion lay in them."[78] Edwards notes that the person began to have such experiences "when a little child of about five or six years of age."[79]

An even more arresting description by Edwards of a child's religious experience is found in his narrative regarding the four-year-old Phebe Bartlet. Phebe had been introduced to the notion of individual salvation by her elder brother (We are explicitly told by Edwards that her parents considered her too young to be educated on this issue). Soon after, Phebe begins "secret prayers" several times a day and moves through a course from fear of hell to an abiding sense of God's love for her.[80] Further, Phebe turns her concern for salvation outwards "for the good of others' souls" and manifests "an uncommon degree of a spirit of charity." Phebe beseeches at length her father to come to the aid of a poor neighbor who is unable to sustain his family.[81]

Historians of American religion have often noted the Great Awakening's re-emphasis on the doctrine of original sin and infant depravity, but have not adequately acknowledged its appreciation of the child's capacity for religious experience. It is recognition of this capacity for intense religious feelings that opened the way for the genuine "sentimentalization" of childhood, and which came to foster a new valuing of persons in this early stage of life.

With the elevation of the mother, children came to be valued for the emotional satisfaction which they offered. In the Christian family, she came to be seen as the more important caretaker religiously, morally and intellectually, and came to displace the father as the primary parent. Even in the more staid, mainstream churches of New England, ministers in the first two decades of the nineteenth century fervently preached of the superiority of maternal parenting abilities and responsibilities. This contradicted, of course, the patriarchal family ideal of earlier times.[82]

With the ascendancy of the mother in the home came the rise of "family sentiment"; affective bonding between parent and child was more greatly emphasized.[83] Jean Jacques Rousseau

(1712-1778) had already castigated the traditional Renaissance notion venerating fathers as the more suited to child rearing: "ambition, avarice, tyranny, the mistaken foresight of fathers, their neglect, their harshness, are a hundredfold more harmful to the child than the blind affection of the mother."[84] English and American romantic poets such as Wordsworth and Emily Dickinson promoted childhood as an ideal state of heart and mind that should be maintained throughout an individual's lifetime. The impact of Romanticism, although immensely diffuse,[85] was not comparable to that of the weekly sermons of preachers on their congregations or to that of the multiplicity of Christian women's organizations, which affirmed mothers in understanding and fulfilling their central parenting role. As women became spiritual leaders within the home and beyond, the affective value of children increased rapidly.

Liberal Christianity of the nineteenth century sided with the Romantics in rejecting the traditional Christian notion of original sin and its corollary of infant depravity. For some Calvinists throughout the nineteenth century, this doctrine meant that many children who died at a very young age, without salvation, would suffer eternal damnation. However, as Peter Slater has noted, even Puritan clergymen of the seventeenth century, when discussing specific children, almost always presumed their destination to be heaven. Moreover, Slater astutely observes that the Romantic view of the flawless, innocent child exalted above all human beings may have also served to further distance adults from flesh and blood children, who almost certainly did not always conform to this ideal type.[86] Slater also notes how the doctrine of Original Sin may have served as a lightning rod for the normal parental feelings of impatience and resentment which cause contemporary parents such guilt or elaborate denial.

Horace Bushnell's *Christian Nurture* was to provide a successful synthesis of Calvinism and liberal Christianity, cognizant of Enlightenment and Romantic concerns. Bushnell maintained a role for divine grace, while at the same time proposing a model which envisioned child rearing as a gradual process of development leading to the mature Christian. Such nurture, according to Bushnell, came less from formal moral and religious teaching than from "the look, the voice, the handling."[87] Bushnell evinces the softening of Protestant theology "and the sentimentalization of northern culture" which social historians have long correlated with the increase of the proportion of women to men in churches.[88]

Also in the nineteenth century, Christians demonstrated concern to varying degrees, not only with the salvation of their children, but also their preparation for worldly success. Evangelical Christians remained convinced of the need for conversion to assure the salvation of children, but the great majority of Christians inclined to a nurture model of child rearing fostering the child's self-realization as responsible Christians and citizens. The caring, affectionate mother was affirmed by conservative and, liberal Christians as the spiritual center of the home and most importantly to the spiritual and material fortunes of children.

Christian women and men of this time also demonstrated their concern for children who were outside the embrace of families. The phenomenon of surplus children abandoned by parents unable or unwilling to support them continued into the nineteenth century in both the United States and Europe.[89] By the last decade of the century in Britain alone, an estimated half million women were involved in philanthropic activities, many of them on behalf of children.[90] In America during the first half of the nineteenth century, abandoned and neglected children were placed in institutions—many of them privately run. By 1850, there was mounting criticism of such institutions and Protestant reformers were prominent in advocating for foster homes.[91] The passage of truancy laws in the 1850s, supported by female Protestant reformers, provided the legal means of forcibly removing from their homes children who were not attending school. Effectively, this allowed Protestant-led organizations to remove children from immigrant Catholic and Jewish families and put them with Protestant foster families. Maureen Fitzgerald has correctly characterized the motivation of Protestant reformers: after having judged "adult Irish to be irredeemable, they also believed removing innocent children from the same immoral environment, especially from their parents, would increase their chances to escape poverty."[92] Thus, the dual Protestant concern to "save" children from material as well as spiritual damnation motivated the placing out of hundreds of thousands of children (by the mid-1870s, 10,000 children per year were "placed out" from New York City alone).[93] Gradually, the Catholic reserve of nuns was to provide an alternative system of care for the children of the Catholic poor. By 1875, there were 1000 nuns working in New York City, and within a decade, the number was to double. These nuns cared for the children of indigent parents, most of whom were returned to their families in better times.[94]

Catholic and Jewish parents ultimately used institutionalization offered by their religious organizations as part of a survival strategy when in financial difficulty. By 1885, nuns directly controlled eighty percent of New York City's public child-care system, housing 15,000 children at a time.[95] According to Fitzgerald, Protestant women, partly in reaction to such Catholic dominance, advocated for direct aid to families with dependent children. Protestant women prevailed in this effort in establishing the modern program of *Aid to Dependent Children*, later to be known as *Aid to Families with Dependent Children* (AFDC)[96] on the grounds that the preservation of the family unit was mandated by concerns for the public good. Of course the "intact" family in question often had only one parent.

The largely Protestant-constructed ideal of the home as a haven, which provided a protected "space" for a childhood free from the corrupting influence of the world, increasingly came to define American children's lives. In the late nineteenth and early twentieth century, a new Christian crusade, which would unite Protestants, Catholics and Jews, was launched to put an end to child labor which violated this new ideal of childhood. In *Crusade for the Children*, Walter Trattner documents the key leadership provided by Christian clergy in opposing child labor in the United States. In 1820, children comprised forty-three percent of the labor force in the textile mills of Massachusetts, forty-seven percent in Connecticut and fifty-five percent in Rhode Island.[97] In 1880, the U.S. Census showed more than one million children between the ages of ten and fifteen were working, and the actual number was, in all likelihood, much higher.[98] Up to the late nineteenth century, a child, not the wife, was more likely to be a family's second wage earner.[99] Yet, by the end of the nineteenth century, the urban middle class had succeeded in constructing the "economically worthless" but emotionally invaluable child.[100] By 1930, lower-class children entered the world of childhood wherein "the sanctity of emotional value of a child made labor taboo."[101] In *Pricing the Priceless Child*, Vivianna Zelizer describes the new conceptualization as a process of "socialization," which she defines as "being invested with sentimental or religious meaning."[102] Thus, child labor came to be seen most importantly as a profanation of a holy thing.

A comparison of the legal criteria for adjudicating wrongful death suits involving children in the nineteenth and twentieth centuries is instructive. In the nineteenth century, American courts calculated the price of the life of a child according to a straightforward formula: "the probable value of services of the deceased less the expense of his maintenance during the same time."[103] Judicial standards explicitly excluded moral and sentimental considerations in such cases. In the late 1920s the now prevalent social attitudes concerning the economically "worthless" but emotionally priceless child clashed with the court's prevailing standard for estimating the "surrender" value of children at death. Between 1920 and 1960, sentimental considerations were accepted in wrongful death lawsuits and were to become the central factor in determining settlements.[104] A 1961 United States Court of Appeals articulated the new judicial standard in accord with the transformed social valuation of the child when it refused to deduct the "projected costs of raising the deceased" seven-year-old boy: "Such cold-blooded deduction...would treat an incalculable loss as a 'pecuniary gain'. What makes life worth living more than the privilege of raising a son?...Is it not still the law in that most sacred of relationships that it is more blessed to give than to receive."[105] Here the court testifies to the triumph of an American Christian campaign sacralizing children which hearkens back to the words of Jesus: "As you did it to one of the least of these my brethren, you did it to me" (Matt 25:40) and "it is more blessed to give than to receive" (Acts 20:35).

As in previous eras, however, the twentieth century reveals no linear path of progress towards an ideal family. Conflicting trajectories have confounded expectations.

The twentieth century began with diminished hope that philanthropy could continue to fulfill its social task, but greatly enhanced confidence in the state's potential contribution to it.[106] However, as the century drew to a close, we paradoxically found several American political leaders, including the president of the nation, imploring churches to assume a greater social role. Why is such advocacy necessary?

Compulsory schooling in the modern world immensely expanded the role of the state in children's lives. Although these schools, at their origins and into the early twentieth century, were heavily influenced by religious educators, leaders and ideas, they have become increasingly secularized. This secularization was not a problem as long as an overwhelming majority of students were exposed also to the moralizing forces of synagogues, churches and "Saturday" or "Sunday Schools." However, such influence has declined along with the institutions exercising it. The current secular emphasis on character education among school leaders is thus an attempt to respond to the consequences of a growing number of youth bereft of the civilizing influences of religion and moral education as provided by family, school or church. Such children from less fortunate circumstances may identify themselves as members of the "Bloods, the Latin Kings, Netas and *La Familia*—street gangs made notorious for their acts of unprovoked violence.[107]

The twentieth century has also seen vast numbers of middle-class and upper-class youth fast become consumer addicts, for whom money is more readily available than caring and loving guidance. As more and more women have entered the work force, the young have lost their primary caretakers and T.V. has come to have an inordinate influence on children's lives. Mass advertising has exploited children's consumer desires, made possible by the historic reversal of the flow of economic goods from children to parent.[108] Moreover, once the egalitarian liberalism of the nineteenth century, which previously informed America's political and economic spheres, was applied to the family, the risk to children posed by contemporary mores heightened. Indeed, children may be the most disadvantaged by their new found "equality."[109] As Zelizer has suggested, the new emotional value of children is predicated on the feelings of their parents, the emotional satisfaction adults derive from children.[110] When such human feelings are not grounded in a religious commitment to transcendent values, the achieved new valuation of the child may indeed prove to be a precarious attainment. Children may be readily seen as obstacles to career success or the couple's marital happiness.[111] Given all this, it should not be surprising to find in the late twentieth century a renewed focus on the family in new, emerging Christian movements as well as mainstream Christianity.

4

Twentieth-Century Christian Efforts to Save the Family

In this chapter, the efforts in the later half of the twentieth century of both the Southern Baptist Convention (SBC) and the Roman Catholic Church to support and strengthen families are explored. Together, the two denominations account for better than one of every three Christians in the nation. While the SBC is the largest Protestant denomination, the Roman Catholic Church in America is almost four times its size. Moreover, these two denominations have generated marriage and family ministries and programs that have been widely adopted/adapted by other mainstream denominations. In this sense, their family ministries are representative of an even greater number of Christians who are engaged in activities supportive of marriage and family.

The SBC has both shaped and been shaped by Southern culture. Perhaps supported by the South's conservative culture, the Southern Baptists have been the least susceptible to the dramatic change of attitudes witnessed in the wider moral environment, especially with respect to sexual issues.[1] At the same time, there can be little doubt that the strenuous efforts of the SBC in upholding traditional family values has played a significant role in sustaining the moral steadfastness of its membership.

American Catholics, on the other hand, have experienced,

over the last four decades, the most radical transformation among all the denominations. During this period, Catholics initially gained parity with Protestants in terms of income and higher education and later surpassed their Protestant brethren.[2] While in 1969, more Catholics disapproved of pre-marital sex than Protestants (72 percent vs. 70 percent), by 1985 only 33 percent of Catholics still believed so while a majority of Protestants continued to disapprove.[3] By way of explanation, several Catholic commentators point to Pope Paul VI's reaffirmation of the traditional ban on artificial birth control in marriage, a re-affirmation which came despite the fact that a full commission established by the Pope voted to drop the ban.[4] With the commission having jettisoned one official teaching, Catholics seemed more ready to deviate from others. Nevertheless, American Catholics remain strongly in agreement with official teachings on extra-marital sex as well as Church doctrine that addresses other sexual issues. In recent years, American Catholics are experiencing something of a religious revival which has engaged the hierarchy, clergy and laity in common causes supportive of marriage and family.

ROMAN CATHOLICISM: MARRIAGE AND FAMILY AS MINISTRY

On specific teachings such as birth control, divorce, and even pre-marital sex, a huge and yawning chasm divides the Catholic hierarchy, including the Pope and many of his bishops, from American Catholic clerics and their parishioners.[5] Nevertheless, at this same time there has been a deep and growing convergence among the papacy, clergy and American Catholic laity in their commitment to develop a family-enabling theology, spiri-

tuality and ministry. Not surprisingly, many of the most significant and enduring Catholic contributions to the family have
been made by Catholic marrieds who have gained significant
recognition and endorsement within the church, often from the
Papacy itself as well as the American hierarchy. Such lay contributions, and certainly their reception by the hierarchy, would
have most probably been inconceivable without the changes initiated by the Second Vatican Council and Pope John XXIII and
his successors.[6]

The most substantial impact of the Second Vatican Council
on American Catholicism was the rise of lay persons in ecclesiastical ministry and leadership.[7] By 1990, the laity overwhelmingly predominated in staffing parish schools and religious
education programs. Given that pragmatism has never been considered a sufficient virtue by the Vatican, the declining numbers
of priests and religious could not alone explain this unprecedented
access to various aspects of parish ministry. Most importantly,
the enhanced roles which persons with families assumed in the
church coincided with an impressive reconstrual by the Vatican
of the meaning of the sacrament of matrimony and the significance of Christian marriage and family, both for the church and
in themselves. A critical point in papal reflection on the family
must date to John XXIII's asseveration that the family is the
"ecclesia domestica," the domestic church.[8] Both Popes Paul VI,
John's immediate successor, and John Paul II have repeated this
designation for the family. Paul VI underscored marriage as "the
primary form of personal communion"[9] and thus began to give
theological grounding to earlier Papal pronouncements, which
had acknowledged that marital sexuality has legitimate purposes
beyond procreation.

Indisputably, it is Pope John Paul II who has given Catholicism the most eloquent and profound expression of the meaning of marriage and family.[10] From the start of his papacy until the present day, John Paul II has frequently written and spoken in depth about marriage and family. Indeed, it is likely that the total volume of his words on the family equals or surpasses the cumulative total of all prior popes. From the outset of his Papacy, John Paul II declared that the intimate union of husband and wife and their children is the decisive community determining the "fate of nations and continents, of humanity and the church."[11] In Kinshasa, Zaire in 1980, he preached to the faithful about the "union of hearts" and warned partners against demanding "to be loved in the same way as he or she loves."[12] Again and again, he has returned to the theme of love as a unique and free gift and, indeed, as having a transcendent source. In an extended treatment on the family in 1981, he spoke loftily of the sacrament of matrimony, which provides the way to live the special "complex of interpersonal relationships."[13] It is the sacrament of matrimony which grants to family members "the dignity and vocation of being really and truly a ministry of the church at the service of the building up of her members."[14] Parents are acknowledged as the "first and foremost educators of their children."[15] He draws the parallel closely between the ministry of parents, the sacrament of matrimony and that of Holy Orders, apparently to encourage both the ministry of parents to their children and the recognition of the similarity between the challenges associated with living in fidelity to one's spouse for life and in being celibate pursuant to vows of perpetual chastity.[16]

John Paul II emphasizes that one important aspect of the educational responsibility that parents have towards their children involves leading them to embrace the virtue of chastity.[17] Without this virtue, the child cannot achieve responsible love.

Beyond premarital abstinence, however, the Pope has spoken on the centrality and blessedness of sexuality which allows parents to "participate" with God in bringing human life into existence.[18] Consistent with this emphasis, all sexual relations, according to official Catholic teachings, are proper only within the bonds of permanent marital commitment:

> Sexuality, by means of which man and woman give themselves to one another through the acts which are proper and exclusive to spouses, is by no means something purely biological, but concerns the innermost being of the human person as such. It is realized in a truly human way only if it is an integral part of the love by which a man and a woman commit themselves totally to one another until death.[19]

The Pope is relentless in his castigation of "free love," which he decries as rarely having all its consequences taken into consideration, including children "condemned to be in fact orphans of living parents."[20] If his affirmations often seem far from contemporary values, including, at times, those of his American flock, he nevertheless reminds his readers of his compassion and motivation:

> From the first years of my priesthood I have become increasingly convinced of this, from when I began to sit in the confessional to serve the concerns, fears and hopes of many married couples. I met difficult cases of rebellion and refusal, but at the same time so many marvelously responsible and generous persons. In writing this letter I have all those married couples in mind and I embrace them with my affection and my prayer.[21]

It appears that many American Catholics do respond to the warm embrace and affection of their Pontiff, and sometimes even his teachings, if in their own way.

In the Catholic church, it is the bishops who are directly subject to the authority of the Pope and who together with him are commissioned to do the "work of Christ the Eternal Pastor."[22] In military terms, the bishops are the commanders responsible for designated regions called dioceses and are accountable directly to the Supreme Commander, the Pope. Over the past two decades, the American bishops have become increasingly vocal in encouraging family ministry, establishing a national infrastructure to provide information, foster research and build associations for those involved in family ministry. In 1978, the National Conference of Catholic Bishops (NCCB) in the United States published "Family Ministry: A Pastoral Plan and a Reaffirmation" which was intended to be a "resource for those who work with families at the diocesan and parish levels."[23] One outcome of the Bishops' family pastoral plan was the formation of the National Association of Catholic Family Life Ministers (NACFLM), begun in 1980 primarily for "those engaged in Marriage Preparation and Enrichment" throughout the Catholic Church in the United States.[24] Acknowledging the expanded role of the laity in the church, the NCCB established the Laity Secretariat in 1977. In 1988, it became the Secretariat for Laity and Family Life with a particular focus on family life, women and youth.[25] The NCCB Committees are comprised of bishops but, importantly, have advisory staffs of lay men and women who have professional expertise. The Committees' publications evidence a concern to encourage pastoral leaders to make family ministry a primary focus of their work as well as to provide "techniques for implementing a family perspective into all policies, programs, ministries and services…"[26] The Committee also publishes some scholarly works such as its 1999 "Marriage Preparation and Cohabiting Couples: An Information Report on New Realities and Pastoral Practices" intended to help marriage and family ministries be more effective.[27]

A focus on marriage preparation is a mainstay of the past and current Catholic marriage and family ministry. Divisional generals may have a great battle strategy, but it is the company field offices who must execute it. Catholic priests have, by and large, enormous spiritual authority in their parishes. In many cases, priests have led the revolt by American Catholics on sexual issues.[28] From a pastoral perspective, parish priests understand themselves to be serving the spiritual and personal needs of their community and protecting its members from the unreasonable intrusions of the Vatican on their marital and family life.[29] There is, however, evidence that the Vatican's unrelenting stand against pre-marital sex is beginning to be heard by parish priests. Jim Bowman quotes a Chicago parish priest involved in marriage preparation classes for his nine-hundred-family church: "In the last three years, there's been a turn around here. To people shacking up together, I have been saying you can't do that and come to this church. We are going back to saying these are the standards. Not necessarily Catholic standards, but according to God's word."[30] Likewise, Charles R. Morris, in *American Catholic: The Saints and Sinners Who Built America's Most Powerful Church*, quotes a Georgetown Jesuit who also works in a young adult parish: "I'm very conservative on sexual issues. Talk all you want about a 'responsible sexual ethic', but as far as I can see from my pastoral work, women are being terribly exploited. The guys move from relationship to relationship and leave a trail of shattered lives."[31] The NCCB's 1999 report "Marriage Preparation and Cohabiting Couples," estimates that almost half the couples who come for marriage preparation in the Catholic Church are in a cohabiting relationship.[32] The report should further encourage the growing conservatism on the part of many Catholic pastors with respect to pre-marital sexuality, as it points to the well-documented increased risks for higher divorce rates among couples who cohabited before marriage, arising from both pre-disposing attitudes and experiences from cohabitation itself.[33]

Michael J. McManus, president of Marriage Savers, Inc. and a practicing Presbyterian, believes the Catholic Church does a better job than any other denomination in preparing couples for marriage.[34] For couples desiring to be married in the Catholic Church, a marriage preparation course is mandatory. Thus, the vast majority of dioceses and parishes offer marriage preparation programs for engaged couples.[35] The quality of such programs has evolved from its earliest form, when it was little more than an interrogation by a priest of engaged persons separately to determine their canonical eligibility to marry in the church.[36] Today, engaged Catholic couples are often offered multi-session programs conducted by a team composed of clergy, lay married couples and parish staff. Indeed, surveys indicate that it is just such team-staffed programs which have the highest perceived value by participants.[37]

Several elements of the church's marriage preparation program have proven effective, including imposing a minimum preparation period of usually four to six months, the use of "prenuptial inventories" and the pairing of engaged couples with older mentor couples. In its February 27, 1995 cover story, *Time* magazine interviewed an engaged couple, Mark Geyman and Laura Richards, who were participating in just such a program.[38] The engaged couple met in four 90-minute sessions with their mentor couple. In their first session they took the "pre-marital inventory" of more than 100 questions, ranging from family size preferences to questions about personal confidence and trust.[39] The mentor couple immediately focused on revealed strains in their relationship involving strong feelings of jealousies which Laura had towards her fiancé's female coworkers. Mark comments in the interview as a result of the meetings with the mentoring couple: "We have done a lot of talking, more than we had." He notes that his fiancée is beginning to "open a little more—she's being more trusting." The opportunity to deal with such hidden fault lines can help significantly improve the quality of marital relations in the initial years. This is attested to by the more than 93 percent of Catholic couples in their first year of marriage who viewed their participation in marriage preparatory programs as valuable.[40] The perceived value of these programs decreases significantly in subsequent years of the marriage, suggesting that "additional proactive supports must be provided to couples" after marriage.[41] Indeed, most parishes devote far fewer resources to the spiritual enrichment of married couples.

Fortunately, however, several Catholic lay movements have at least partially filled the gap over the past fifty years. Already in the 1940s, two significant Catholic family movements were born in the United States whose ministries extended beyond the direct control of parish clergy: The Cana Conference and the Christian Family Movement (CFM).[42] Begun as a men's Catholic Action group in 1943 in Chicago and transformed into a couples' organization by 1946, the CFM focused on larger social forces, which were understood to be contrary to a Christian social order as well as family life. By 1963, more than 40,000 couples in the United States and Canada were actively participating in biweekly meetings, typically in groups of five or six families, to discuss spiritual and social action issues. By the late 1960s, however, the movement was flagging, strained perhaps by its dual focus on family spirituality and social action.[43] Vestiges of the CFM survive in many Catholic parishes today, although they are as likely to be hosting a "renewal of vows ceremony" for married couples as staging social protests.[44]

Focused on the internal renewal of families, the Cana Conference began from a retreat for married couples in St. Louis,

Missouri in October, 1944. The retreat was conducted by a Jesuit, Edward Dowling, who explained its purpose as learning to apply religious principles to the mundane aspects of marital life.[45] Unlike the typical Catholic retreat of the time, the Cana format was held in a hall in an informal and relaxed atmosphere, where there was an attempt to address the particular spiritual concerns and needs of modern American families. This movement quickly mushroomed, proliferating not only its retreats for married couples, but also developing a Pre-Cana conference for engaged couples. This was the precursor of the Catholic marriage preparation courses discussed previously. The movement also contributed to the development of religious education programs for high school students and adults. This movement stimulated thousands of clergy and lay persons to become engaged in marriage and family ministry as well as the appointment of Family Life Directors in most U.S. dioceses.

As the Cana Movement was waning in the late 1960s, a powerful new movement arose, again from the Catholic laity, Marriage Encounter. The enormous impact which this movement has had on Catholic families is suggested by the testimonials which are available on its Web site. These include the affirmation of Pope John Paul II: "I place much of my hope for the future in Marriage Encounter."[46]

Some two million American couples have participated in Marriage Encounter weekend retreats, and studies show that 80 to 90 percent of those attending "literally fall back in love."[47] The intent of the weekend is to give married couples the opportunity to learn a "technique of loving communication that they can use the rest of their lives."[48] Participant couples hear a series of talks from lead couples and after each talk write answers to given questions. The couple then read each other's answers and engage in discussion. The emphasis of the weekend is on communication between husbands and wives.

Marriage Encounter now involves more than a dozen denominations which have adapted the program in accord with their specific spiritual orientation. Interestingly, Marriage Encounter has designed its weekend program so that priests and religious can also participate: "The principles of love, commitment and effective communication translate quite readily to the relationship between priest and his parish or any group to whom he ministers as well as to a religious community."[49] This movement may have made accessible experientially John Paul II's insight about the parallels in the sacraments of Holy Orders and Matrimony. After a Marriage Encounter weekend, which clergy also attended, one couple affirmed that they recognized "the similarity of our sacraments."[50] Through a Marriage Encounter weekend, many couples find a community of "like-minded couples with similar values about Christian marriage" and also sometimes clergy with whom they can readily relate.[51]

Marriage Encounter also gave birth to a second program, Retrouvaille, after its leaders in Quebec asked a few couples who attended the weekend why they still were getting divorced. The unsuccessful Marriage Encounter participants expressed their sentiments that their problems were more serious than poor communication and involved issues such as many years of adultery.[52] In response the Quebec Marriage Encounter couples created a more intensive weekend retreat, Retrouvaille, to save marriages headed for divorce. In these weekends the veteran couples who had rebuilt marriages after adultery, alcoholism or abuse share openly how they overcame their problems and serve as mentors to attending couples. By 1996, Retrouvaille was holding weekends in a hundred metro areas in the United States and had saved the marriages of 80 percent of the nearly 50,000 couples who had attended them.[53] McManus expresses the central idea behind this and other marriage-saving programs simply: "Every church has a marriage-saving resource in its pews—couples who have built rewarding, lifelong marriages. They can help other couples do the same." It seems possibly the Catholic Church has utilized this resource more as a result of its celibate American priests having turned over its marriage preparation programs to older couples some thirty years ago.

Already by 1987, George Gallup, Jr. and Jim Castelli had concluded that a religious revival was taking place in the American Catholic Church.[54] When canvassing the percentage of Catholics taking part in religious activities outside the church in 1977 and then in 1986, they found that almost 4 percent of them had made a retreat in 1986 vs. 1 percent in 1977, and that 3 percent had attended a spiritual conference vs. 1 percent in 1977. The percentage of those attending a Marriage Encounter session, however, had decreased from 4 percent in 1977 to 2 percent in 1986. Thus a significantly higher percentage were attending explicitly spiritual retreats and conferences in 1986 compared to 1977, yet at the same time, the percentage of people attending Marriage Encounter weekends had decreased by 50 percent. Some American Catholics seemed to be looking for a decidedly more spiritual approach to even marital and family matters.

The ever increasing Hispanic presence in the American Catholic Church has undoubtedly also had an impact. In 1994, Alex Garcia-Rivera could proudly proclaim in *U.S. Catholic*, "the Hispanic Catholic home altar is truly a custom for all Catholic families today. The signs of the times are that a struggle for the Catholic family is taking place. The home altar ought to mark the battlefront of that struggle as a sign of bold faith."[55] Garcia-Rivera recalls fondly his family gathering at the altar in his home in Cuba, praying the rosary and singing Christmas songs; this is the one import that Garcia-Rivera is happily willing to allow into the U.S., and there may be more than a few interested American Catholics.

In 1989, the 850-acre Catholic Familyland campus opened in the remote Allegheny foothills of eastern Ohio. Since then, the campus has enrolled thousands of Catholic parents and their children in three- to five-day "spiritual boot camps."[56] The founders of Familyland, Jerry Coniker and his wife and several children, began a lay Apostolate for Family Consecration in 1975 in Kenosha, Wisconsin,[57] a program which encourages Catholic families to consecrate their families to Christ through Mary in union with Joseph. The Apostolate produces thousands of video tapes, cassette tapes, books, compact disks and CD-Roms which encourage families to pray, and specifically, to build their relationship with the Holy Family. Coniker calls Familyland a spiritual detox center for families: "Here they can obtain the tools of evangelization…there are no Walkmans here, no TV, no radio, no liquor. Just time to let God, nature and the family work together."[58] Father Kevin Barrett, the Chaplain of Catholic Familyland, is even more direct about the spiritual purpose of the camp: "to teach families how to take up arms against an enemy trying to destroy them; that enemy is Satan himself and his minions (i.e. fallen angels) who work night and day to plot our ruin…to destroy holiness, marriage and the purity and innocence of youth."[59] Barrett sees much of contemporary media, especially rock music, television, magazines and newspapers, as the modern demonic "tools of warfare." The Apostolate encourages families to make a 54-day rosary novena. According to

Barrett "hell's going to be trembling from the power rising up in your home if you do."[60]

Using videos, by 1997, the Apostolate was facilitating more than 400 group meetings in private homes in what it calls "Peace of Heart Forums." These foster discussion, faith-sharing and support. All levels of the Catholic hierarchy seem supportive of Catholic Familyland as Curia cardinals, Vatican officials, U.S. bishops and numerous clergy visit Catholic Familyland on a regular basis.[61]

In the face of criticism, both internal and external, concerning the alleged impenetrable lines of hierarchy of the Catholic Church, it is, indeed, remarkable how the Catholic family movement has so often crossed over these lines. American clergy, bishops and even the Pope have warmly endorsed and embraced several Catholic lay family movements from the Cana movement and CFM to Marriage Encounter and Catholic Familyland. There can be little doubt that in the twenty-first century a decisive requirement for the spiritual health of all Catholics will be the further integration in church ministry of the creative energy and spirituality of its most gifted families. Assuming that is the case, however, the Catholic Church should continue to contribute greatly to the health and happiness of its families, and the well-being of our nation.

THE SOUTHERN BAPTIST CONVENTION: PROVIDING RESOURCES TO STRENGTHEN FAMILIES

Over the last two-thirds of the twentieth century, the Southern Baptist Convention (SBC) has evinced a growing awareness of the family as a prime focus for ministry. Three stages in the development of the SBC's concern for the family can be discerned.

From 1940-1960, the primary intent was to encourage individual members of the family—husbands, wives and children—to embrace and practice the basic disciplines of discipleship: prayer, Bible study and worship in the home and at church.[62] In the second period, from 1960-1980, Southern Baptists developed both a biblically grounded theology of the family[63] and the beginnings of a professional quality family ministry for church families.[64] In the third stage, from 1980 to the present, the SBC has increasingly engaged wider cultural forces, which it perceives as inimical to traditional family values and has become both directly and indirectly a powerful champion of such values on the national scene. Needless to say, the perspectives and approaches of earlier stages are not necessarily eliminated in later periods. Certainly the call for individual devotion continues to be sounded in the present period by the Southern Baptist leadership.

In *Baptist History and Heritage*, Reuben Herring mused that if the resolutions concerning family life adopted by the SBC in 1980 were any indication, "the 1980s may well become the Decade of the Family."[65] Herring's forecast in terms of the centrality of the concern for family by the SBC was accurate, and the same could even more accurately be said of the 1990s, as the focus intensified through the end of the century.

The SBC first gave focused attention to family ministry at its 1937 annual meeting, when the Training Union study course book, *Building a Christian Home*, by Martha Boone Leavell, was published.[66] Its emphasis on spiritual matters as the solution to family problems was reflected further in the denomination's newly published (1938) quarterly magazine, *The Better Home*. The journal expressed its mission to publish poetry, fiction and articles which contribute to a "goal of creating a family atmosphere con-

ducive to spiritually committed lives and to assist Baptist homes
in being better homes."[67] Significantly, at the 1940 SBC annual
meeting, it was recommended that churches set aside May 4-11,
1941 on the denominational calendar to observe Christian Home
Week.[68] Citing the positive response, the Sunday School Board,
through its Training Union Department, requested and received
approval from the SBC to continue Home Week.[69] By 1945, the
circulation of *The Better Home* had climbed to 125,000. The
Sunday School Board was sensing a whole new area of mission:
"Perhaps the most undeveloped field of service open to our
churches is a vital ministry to Christian homes."[70]

Immediately after the end of World War II, Joe W. Burton
was made editor of the home curriculum of the Sunday School
Board. In Burton, Southern Baptists had a strong and capable
advocate of family ministry receptive to the social sciences and
family studies as well as the biblical and theological heritage.[71]
In 1947, Burton became editor of *Home Life,* which has remained
the most significant periodical for Southern Baptists promoting
Christian family life.[72] The magazine was a success from its start,
with over three million copies issued in the first year. In 1948,
the SBC made the important decision that family ministry, like
evangelism, would belong to *all* departments of the Sunday
School Board, underscoring the denomination's increasing commitment to enhancing the quality of Christian family life.[73]
Throughout most of the 1950s, the focus of the Home Curriculum Department was to continue to provide spiritually uplifting material that would help churches inspire members to a
healthy family life and family worship experiences in which
Southern Baptists would pray, read Scripture and share God's
grace at home.[74]

By the end of the 1950s, the Home Curriculum Department was developing plans to co-sponsor a marriage and family counseling center with Southwestern Baptist Theological Seminary.[75] In 1961, John Drakeford opened a family counseling center for students at Southwestern, in which he developed family life counseling as a discipline distinct from the pastoral counseling approach.[76] In the same year, the Home Curriculum Department changed its name to the Family Life Department and expanded its responsibilities to include training family life education leaders, whose mission was to coordinate regional family ministry workshops and conduct research. William Clemmons, in 1971, became the supervisor of the Family Ministry and Vocational Guidance Committee and hired trained family counselors who "moved Baptist family ministry toward providing professional quality services for church families."[77] Throughout the 1970s, skilled family counselors were employed by the SBC; these counselors conducted workshops, planned Family Ministry Weeks and assisted with an annual series of age-graded books for use during Christian Home Week.[78]

Perhaps some reaction to this professionalism of family ministry was inevitable within the SBC leadership. While Secretary of the Family Ministry Department of the Sunday School Board, Joseph W. Hinkle wrote in early 1980: "Baptists must declare a moratorium on chasing after the newest psychological model as a final answer to the family life dilemma, and fervently advocate the radical and revolutionary teachings of Jesus on the family."[79] Already in the 1970s, there were a series of volleys from the SBC sounding a battle cry against the macro-cultural forces hostile to marriage as a lifelong monogamous commitment and to other traditional family values. Increasingly, Southern Baptists came to feel that the secular values of American mainstream culture were in conflict with Christian family values. In 1975, with a broad resolution on marriage and family, the SBC praised the family as the source of peace, prosperity and spiritual well-being for the nation and criticized the media for presenting unhealthy models.[80] This resolution further urged the SBC to proclaim monogamy as Christ's teaching as well as to provide "compassionate help for couples with marital problems." Indeed, the 1980s saw Southern Baptists mobilizing their greatest efforts yet to help families; its 1982-1985 Bold Mission Thrust "Strengthen Families" emphasis called upon every church to provide help and resources for families to deepen their spiritual foundations.[81] The project, "Family: Opening the Word Together," helped families by providing material for families to study the Bible and worship in the home.[82] Another project, "Marriage: Growing Into Oneness" sought to strengthen family life by helping couples commit themselves to personal and spiritual growth together.[83]

The 1990s, to be sure, witnessed the SBC stepping into the ring to do battle with the forces which it believed were establishing a culture contrary to Christian family values. From 1979, fundamentalist groups within the SBC began assuming dominance over convention boards and agencies.[84] Although various interpretations have been rendered as to why fundamentalists have so solidly locked up positions of power in the SBC,[85] it appears that the fundamentalists best represented the traditional family values of the vast majority of Southern Baptist church goers. Nor can the enormous energy of the Southern Baptist battle for traditional family values be fully explained as merely a conservative reaction to an emerging social scientific, professionally oriented and theologically sophisticated family ministry. As early as 1977, the SBC spoke out against the "new morality" and voiced opposition to the distribution of "information, medication and supplies furnished" to unmarried, minor-aged children without parental consent.[86] In the late 1990s, the SBC decided to target the Disney Company as a symbol of the new culture and voted to boycott Disney products.[87] At the 1997 convention, SBC President Tom Elliff compared supporting Disney to associating with a prostitute and called the company "a purveyor of pornography."[88] Disney may have especially raised the ire of traditional family values advocates due to their sense of having been betrayed by the company's deviation from its founding mission and ideals. In any event, the SBC at the 1997 convention did more than lambaste Disney; it also created a new North American Mission Board (NAMB) which merged the Home Mission Department and the Radio-Television Commission.[89] NAMB has been active in providing alternative electronic entertainment for viewers (see below). At the annual meeting of the SBC in 1998, delegates (called messengers) overwhelmingly approved the adoption of a statement on the family, defining it as "composed of persons related to one another by marriage, blood or adoption."[90] Marriage was reaffirmed as a lifelong union of a man and a woman. The four paragraphs on the family approved at the annual meeting became "officially the 18th article in The Baptist Faith and Message, a pivotal theological text."[91]

The SBC has invested enormously in technological communications, television, radio and, most recently, the Internet, offering through these media an impressive array of resources friendly and supportive to families in the 1990s. The SBC initiated FamilyNet in 1988, which is a twenty-four-hour programming service owned and operated presently by the NAMB of the SBC's Broadcast Communications Group.[92] FamilyNet offers quality family programs whose target audience is described as "the more than 70 million people who feel the family is the most important part of their lives" and are looking for a "wholesome alternative to standard television fare."[93] FamilyNet distributes its programs by satellite to broadcast stations which carry them either part of or the entire day. FamilyNet programs such as "Nana Puddin" and "Kids on the Move" are for children from toddler to pre-teens. Teenagers are offered programs such as "In Your Face" and "Straight Talk From Teens" as well as various Christian music programs. Sports (hunting and fishing), "Classic Money" and "Swan's Place" are a few of the programs intended for all ages. Several programs are specifically designed to elevate family relations such as the "Family Enrichment Series," "Just for Parents" and "Cope." FamilyNet and *Home Life* magazine have cooperated to produce the "Home Life" television program, a half-hour daily series focusing on healthy lifestyles, family values and wholesome relationships within the home. "HomeLife" for television balances celebrity guests with lesser known heroes who have "inspiring stories to share."[94] The producers describe the program as follows: "While a Christian show, it is not issues-oriented or 'churchy' in flavor—guests and segment possibilities are diverse—all with a soft approach."[95] They do, however, distinguish the program from secular talk shows: "our guests not only share their stories, talents, or expert information, but they also have the opportunity to share the role their faith plays in their lives and careers."[96] "HomeLife" is emblematic of how the SBC has continued to innovate while maintaining a consistent spiritual concern to strengthen Christian families in the last half of the twentieth century.

The NAMB has also created "HelpLink," an Internet source of information and advice on family issues. The NAMB coordinates the efforts of "thousands of cooperating local Southern Baptist churches" in the United States who contribute to "HelpLink."[97] The major headings on the "HelpLink" homepage include the following: "Abuse," "Addictive Behaviors," "Financial and Employment Issues," "Family Issues/Parenting," "Marriage and Divorce," "Sexual Behavior" and "Sexual Identity."[98] The Web site carries a disclaimer that the reader should not assume that its documents are substitutes for professional counseling as provided by "mental health professionals, legal counselors or religious practitioners."[99] At the same time, the site boldly affirms "HelpLink offers hope through Jesus Christ. Whatever need a person may have, we believe answers can be found in Jesus."[100] An investigation of the site shows that the advice can be quite practical and down to earth. Under the primary heading "Family Issues/Parenting" for instance, one finds such topics as "Constructive Discipline," "Helping Your Children Cope with Their Fears," "Tips on Achieving Better Grades," "Coping with Strict Parents," "Coping with Unloving Parents," "Leading Your Teens to Independence," "Living with Adult Children" and "Living with a Stepparent."[101] It appears in these sites that every attempt is made to address the real problems of people from a biblical perspective, providing useful and helpful advice.

This is particularly true for topics not commonly associated with an organization like the SBC. For instance, visitors to the site "Sexual Response in Marriage" are encouraged to seek advice from professionals as well as Scripture if they are not achieving a satisfying sexual relationship in their marriages.[102] The site affirms that "sex is intended by God to be a beautiful expression of love and unity" in marriage.[103] Contrary sentiments of repulsion, embarrassment, reticence or sexual dysfunction are discussed as obstacles to be overcome on the road to full marital bliss. The site further advises readers to learn about the physiological and affective dimensions of sex as well as directly what is pleasurable to their own spouse. In a site entitled "Impotence and Marital

Intimacy", the observation is made that men who have had a variety of sexual partners sometimes have a "hang-up about enjoying sex in marriage."[104] The suggestion is continued: "They may have the subconscious idea that sex is dirty or wrong, something you do with 'bad girls', and thus they feel guilty if they have sex with their wives."[105] The focus of the site is to understand the problem and offer effective spiritual and practical solutions, including seeking professional help if necessary.

In the site "A Christian Perspective on Sex", the reader is informed that "God wants persons to have a good sex life…" and to help make "this area of life as pleasurable and rewarding as possible."[106] The site further avers that "God's plan for the use of our sexuality can rightly be called 'maximum sex'"[107] and asserts that such sexuality can only be achieved in the context of a loving marital relationship with God at its center. In its site "Sex in Dating: Setting Limits", readers are told that dating should be "primarily a social activity," not a sexual one.[108] Recognizing that a "barrage of sexual images and explicit sexual portrayals" assault their readers through the entertainment media and advertisement, "HelpLink" acknowledges it is very difficult for people, "especially teenagers and young adults", to make wise choices.[109] The reader is advised to prepare for a date "by making a conscious decision how you will handle sexual temptation before you are in an emotionally heavy situation."[110]

The SBC, however, has been giving more than advice in helping young people remain chaste before marriage. In the late 1980s, the SBC's Sunday School Board prepared a curriculum for Christian sex education which elicited a great response from parents and teenagers seeking further guidance on abstinence.[111] In April 1993, the SBC unveiled the "True Love Waits" campaign to promote biblical sexuality and premarital abstinence for teens. At the 1994 SBC Annual Convention in Orlando, Florida, more than 100,000 signed chastity cards were displayed on the lawn outside the meeting site.[112] In Washington, D.C. at the Capitol Mall, 211,163 signed abstinence pledges were placed on July 29, 1994. On Valentine's Day 1996, over 340,000 teenagers expressed publicly their commitment to remain abstinent as their stacked pledge cards reached from the ground to the roof of the 27-story Georgia Dome.[113] Southern Baptists had succeeded in using peer pressure to affirm a teenage sexual abstinence campaign, and in doing so, demonstrated that biblical sexual values can be sustained in contemporary America.

The SBC stands among white Protestant denominations as a premier pro-family advocate. Some view the SBC's pro-family policy commitments and many activities supportive of families as a natural outgrowth of the Convention's domination since 1980 by Fundamentalists. Others attribute the SBC's seeming preoccupation with family issues to the Southern culture with which it is historically and intimately related. Such factors are not to be discounted. Perhaps most importantly, however, is the intensity of religious beliefs and practices among the general membership of Southern Baptists[114] who are the reservoir of energy and creativity sustaining the mighty flow of family-supportive literature, radio and television programming as well as multitudinous Web sites, which have poured forth from them in the last half-century.

In the following chapter we will examine the contributions of three new religious movements whose very emergence, in large part, was influenced by concerns surrounding the family in modernity.

5

New Religious Movements and the Family

T he three religious movements discussed below are currently highly visible proponents of traditional family life which offer remedies to modernity's well-recognized family malaise. Each of these movements has been, or is still, considered controversial by segments of the wider public; indeed, the self-understanding of each of these movements is radical, seeking to return to an earlier, ideal time or to a promised time never yet realized. Mormonism, the oldest of the three, has its origins in the revelatory experiences of Joseph Smith, dating from the 1800s. The Unification Church originates during the turbulent period of World War II and the subsequent Korean War. It became the most prominent of the new religious movements in the United States in the 1970s. Finally, the Promise Keepers, the youngest of the three movements, was founded in 1990 by Bill McCartney, a prominent football coach who became a born-again Christian. The Promise Keepers focuses on empowering men to accept their responsibility as faithful husbands and fathers. Despite their diverse origins, each of these movements represents, in the twentieth century, a continuation of the history of support that religion has lent to family prosperity.

Conservative religious groups in the United States have experienced exponential membership growth over the last few decades, while membership in liberal, mainstream denominations was steadily declining. The conservative Christian groups have reaffirmed the traditional roles of fathers and husbands within the family and appear to be calling a halt to or even reversing the feminization trend that we have mentioned previously (see Chapter 2). The three new religious movements discussed here may also be interpreted as reacting to the displacement of fathers/ husbands in the home and church. However, they are also distinctive in offering theological innovations with respect to family and marriage (Latter-day Saints and Unification Church) and/ or in exhibiting a heightened commitment to visions of ecumenical and racial unity (the Promise Keepers and Unification Church).

MORMONISM: "FROM 'PURITAN' POLYGAMY TO EXEMPLARY MONOGAMY"

The Church of Latter-day Saints (LDS or also known as Mormonism) has been rightly acknowledged for its contributions to strengthening the traditional monogamous American family in the twentieth century. Theodore Roosevelt observed that Mormon monogamous families adhered to a "standard of morality higher than most."[1] He noted among Mormons there was "less prostitution, less sexual degradation, and less evidence of birth control" than among their neighbors.[2] During his 1980 Presidential election campaign, Ronald Reagan paid similar homage to Mormonism for fostering strong and healthy families in America.

Such praise is all the more noteworthy when one recalls that throughout most of the nineteenth century and into the first decade of this century, Mormons were widely criticized, and even prosecuted, for practicing polygamy in violation of both the nation's marital laws and a growing public sentiment that healthy, monogamous families were the well-spring of and necessary to the health of Western civilization. Up until the second decade of the twentieth century, Mormonism was readily identified with polygamy.[3]

How serious was the Mormon experiment with polygamy, and how is it that Mormonism was able to reverse its perceived role from great destroyer of the monogamous family to one of its greatest advocates? Any attempt to answer these questions must include an examination of the nature and extent of polygamy among Mormon families.

Joseph Smith (1805-1844) and his followers understood themselves to be recapitulating, or reliving, the stories of Israel and early Christianity.[4] Significant events of Israel's past were to be repeated by the Mormons so that, most importantly, the ancient Israelite priestly authority could be recovered by the community of Latter-day Saints. Not surprisingly, the domestic relations of the patriarchs, including Abraham and Jacob as well as the biblical Kings David and Solomon, all of whom were polygamous, provided a pattern for Smith and his followers beginning in Kirtland, Missouri.[5] Further, Joseph Smith and other nineteenth-century Mormon leaders were both aware and critical of the diminished authority of fathers in the American home.[6] Counterbalancing this, within Mormon teachings, every worthy male above the age of twelve was considered to be a member of the Aaronic or the Melchizedek priesthood.[7] The sacerdotal status attributed to Mormon men enhanced their spiritual authority in the household.

Beyond the recovery of patriarchal family life, Mormon leaders offered a plethora of reasons for plural marriages. In 1852,

Mormons proclaimed to the world that they were practicing polygamy.[8] At the same time as this proclamation, the Mormons began a campaign to educate and convert the public on the issue.[9] First and foremost, Mormonism affirmed that Joseph Smith received revelation that "celestial marriage" entailed plural marriage. God had commanded Smith and his followers to enter into polygamous unions. Second, and also based on the revelation warrant, was the scriptural authority for the practice, especially that offered by the examples of Old Testament Patriarchs. Third, Mormonism presented a host of social and moral rationales for polygamy, heavily based on its critique of the contemporary American family and sexual practices.

In their defense of polygamy, nineteenth-century Mormons argued that polygamy was a practical remedy for contemporary social ills. The widespread infidelity by husbands in monogamous marriages could only be overcome by a polygamy in which husbands supported their plural wives and provided for all their children. Mormons readily accepted the prevalent nineteenth-century view of women as asexual and men as highly sexed, finding in this view evidence of nature's preference for polygamy.[10] Mormon apologists also contended that plural marriage was the only means to eliminate prostitution. Further, it was claimed that the number of females exceeded that of males, so that the only way to assure every woman a husband, home and children was through polygamous unions.[11]

Such social reasons were, no doubt, secondary to the Mormons' religious commitment. Following the revelatory pronouncement of their founder Joseph Smith, Mormons believed that the highest glory in the afterlife was reserved for those who entered into polygamous relationships.[12] M. R. Werner, a biographer of Brigham Young, the successor to Joseph Smith who followed Smith's practice of plural marriage, coined the phrase "Puritan polygamy."[13] Mormons practiced polygamy because they believed it to be God's will, necessary to build the Kingdom of God on Earth; further, such plural marriages would, according to Mormon teachings, continue in the afterlife.[14] It was such conviction that underlay Mormon willingness to endure considerable persecution and even prosecution for polygamy; at least one thousand were imprisoned for polygamy between 1888 and 1890.

The widespread depiction of lecherous Mormon men copulating wildly with myriad wives is wide of the mark. Perhaps, in part as a reaction to the charge of sexual profligacy, Mormons began restricting sexual activity to reproductive purposes. From the 1840s until the early twentieth century, Mormons warned against sexual relations when mothers were carrying or nursing children.[15] Reproduction became the sole justification for sexual activity between the marital couple. Assuming such a limitation, the Mormon criticism of monogamy as damming up "the natural channels God created for male sexual expression" became more explicable.[16] However, a Mormon husband with even two or three wives might indeed engage in sexual intercourse less frequently than a faithful monogamous male who did not so restrict the purpose of marital sexual activity.

B. Carmon Hardy concluded that between twenty and thirty percent of all Mormons were living in polygamous families between 1850 and 1890.[17] Moreover, the practice was much more extensive with Mormon leaders at all levels, including those presiding over the entire church. During the time the principle of plural marriage was practiced, tens of thousands of men, women and children lived in Mormon polygamous households and constituted "the most serious challenge to traditional family life in centuries."[18] The American public and its political, religious and news leadership perceived Mormonism as an enemy to the American way of life, and in particular, its tradition of monogamous family life.

In the late nineteenth century, the crusade against Mormonism intensified, culminating in civil rulings to disenfranchise Mormons. The Utah Commission in 1880 barred polygamists from voting.[19] By 1890, national legislature was under consideration to deny the right to vote to all members of the church: on September 24, 1890, then Mormon President Woodruff issued his manifesto instructing all church members to obey the laws of the land with respect to marriage, explicitly rejecting polygamy.[20] Nevertheless, despite this proclamation against plural marriage, around 1899, several Mormon leaders, including the then President of the Church, Joseph F. Smith, were indicted for polygamy.[21] The fact that Mormons including President Smith himself continued to practice polygamy after the 1890 manifesto suggests the reluctance with which many Mormons met the mandated change to a monogamous lifestyle.

The definitive end of the Mormon Church's endorsement of polygamy is to be found in President Joseph F. Smith's new manifesto of 1904. The causes of this relinquishment of polygamous marriage have been variously explained.

Mormonism underwent a profound cultural transformation between 1870 or 1880 and 1920, such that mainstream American values and Mormon values began to converge.[22] While Carmon Hardy chronicles the Mormon retreat from polygamy in stages, linking these stages to increasingly severe government sanctions, or threats thereof, from 1880 to the church's final capitulation in 1904, others hold a different view. Certainly, a prominent perspective, articulated by Klaus Hansen, holds that the Latter-day Saints gave up plural marriage "…as much from an internal response to modernization as from external pressure."[23] Even if one accepts the higher end of the estimated percentage of Mormons involved in polygamous relationships, as of the mid-to-late 1800s, at least 70 percent of the Saints practiced monogamy; thus, from about 1870, many Mormons are understood to have been passively resisting polygamy. Further, Hansen appreciates the genuinely religious character of the early Mormon commitment to polygamy. This central source of power for the practice of plural marriages should not be underestimated. By the same token, however, the Mormon conviction in continuing revelation may have also found believers more open to radical revisions of their own teachings than has been the case with most historical traditions. Their belief in continuing revelation allowed Mormonism the freedom to reassess its original understanding.

Joseph Smith's vision of "celestial marriage" emphasized the central and overriding importance of the principle of plural marriage.[24] As Mormonism in the latter part of the nineteenth century gradually moved away from polygamy, this vision was reinterpreted: the innovative Mormon concept of marriage as an eternal relationship persisting in the spirit world after death displaced the principle of plural marriage. According to Hardy, the notion of "sealing" couples together for eternity was one of the last and most mature developments of Joseph Smith's thought.[25] For Smith, the notion of sealing and the eternity of marriage necessitated polygamy, as in the case of a remarried widower who will be reunited eternally in the afterlife both with his first wife and later spouses. Sealing binds husbands, wives and children to each other eternally; the sealing ceremony can be conducted within the sacred space of the temple, not only for the living, but also for the dead.

By the first decade of the twentieth century, however, Smith's 1843 revelation on celestial marriage was interpreted as having to do primarily with the eternity of marriage and not polygamy.[26] By 1919, official Mormonism could affirm "the propriety of each man having only one wife…and the equation of celestial marriage with a monogamous union for eternity."[27] Although this reversal is dramatic, it should be remembered that the religious motivation as well as moral guidelines for Mormon plural marriages provided the collective impetus for this self-correction, as well as for the frequent Mormon attainment of exemplary monogamous families both before and after the reforms.

The well-known profile of a Mormon culture based on successful monogamous families is rightly deserved. The success of the Mormon family, however, has much to do with Mormon teachings of the importance of family as the eternal unit of salvation. Larry L. Jensen and Ronald Jackson have pointed to the fact that since 1950, the top leadership of the church has stressed the topics of family, marriage and parenthood.[28] This emphasis on spousal and parental caring, exhibited by the leadership in their most important General Conference, is a reaction to a perceived inordinate concern for material success expressed by American families. In the latter half of this century, many such families no longer find wives and mothers raising children but rather engaged equally with their husbands in bread-winning activities. Mormons, who generally approve of material success, have considered that the balance between such success and family care and nurture has been upset. In response to this perceived imbalance, the Latter-day Saints have redoubled their efforts to promote close and loving families as their highest goal. In 1964, Church President David O. McKay stated that "no other success can compensate for failure in the home."[29] His successor, President Harold B. Lee, proclaimed in 1974 "the most important of the Lord's work you will ever do will be the work you do within the walls of your own home."[30]

The Mormon hierarchy has advocated for the preservation of traditional roles of father as provider and mother as nurturer: "By design, fathers are to preside over their families in love and righteousness and are responsible to provide the necessities of life and protection for their families. Mothers are primarily responsible for the nurture of their children. In these sacred responsibilities, fathers and mothers are obligated to help one another as equal partners..."[31] This 1995 Official Proclamation of the Church's First Presidency also reflects an increasing focus on encouraging fathers to be more active within the family. In 1987, Mormon President Ezra Taft Benson addressed Latter-day Saint fathers pointing out that "...while mothers play an important role as the head of the home, this in no way lessens the equally important role fathers should play in nurturing, training, and loving their children."[32] Benson, in this same address, spoke of the husband's responsibility to love one wife, quoting a Mormon scripture which reads "thou shalt love thy wife with all thy heart and shalt cleave unto her and none else." President Benson went on to explain: "To my knowledge, there is only one other thing in all scripture that we are commanded to love with all our hearts and that is God Himself...nothing except God Himself takes priority over your wife in your life—not work, not recreation, not hobbies."[33] In an era of widespread family collapse and cultural confusion, such a religious orientation and high valuing of the husband-wife relationship undoubtedly accounts for the oft-noted and distinctive healthy contemporary Mormon family.

THE UNIFICATION CHURCH: FROM CO-ED MONASTICISM TO A WORLD OF BLESSED FAMILIES

Mary Bednarowski has remarked on the meaning of the family for Mormonism and the Unification Church: "In each movement, the family is not just a contractual, social unit, but an institution which is essential for salvation."[34]

Unlike either Mormonism or the Promise Keepers movement, the Unification Church does not originate in the United States, but rather in East Asia; its founder, Sun Myung Moon, was born in what is now known as North Korea and holds citizenship from South Korea.[35] As the concern of this study is the impact of Christianity (and its derivatives) on the Western family, especially the American family, my comments on the Unification Church here are restricted to its American presence.

Sun Myung Moon and his family moved to the United States in 1972. While he is reportedly presently focusing his ministry in South America, he continues to maintain an oft-visited residence here.[36] Over the four or five years after his arrival in the United States the Rev. Moon personally mobilized a then small number of communalized, relatively sedate Unification members into highly effective evangelizing and money-making teams. This mobilization catapulted his movement into the American national limelight, as the then most successful of the new religions, most often pejoratively called cults.[37] Over the next two decades, this movement would continue to undergo several more transformations in its crusade to offer what it understood as God's original marriage blessing to couples of the world, and to lead those couples to establish "true" God-centered families.

What are the family ideals and practices of Unificationists? A Catholic sociologist, Joseph H. Fichter, has suggested that

Unificationists view marriage much like Catholic nuns and priests look at their career of permanent celibacy, namely from the perspective of a life-long vocation.[38] Throughout the 1960s and 70s, American Unificationists, the majority young people in their twenties, lived in communal centers. Fichter described the familial goal of these centers: "they develop a family relationship looking across sex lines as brothers and sisters. There is a spiritual kinship of agape, close-knit camaraderie and group support within the residence. Selfishness is a serious personal fault. Christian love is the key word..."[39] The sexual mores in these communities could not be more distant from the free-sex communes of the hippie movement. Frederick Sontag described these Unification communities as practicing a "co-ed monasticism" wherein all pre-marital and extra-marital sex was strictly taboo.[40] There also remains a definitive difference between the Unification communities and Catholic monasticism, in that the former practice a temporary celibacy in order to prepare for life-long, even eternal, marriage.

According to Rev. Moon's interpretation of the biblical fall story, Adam and Eve prematurely had a sexual relationship which God had fully intended them to enjoy, but only after reaching spiritual maturity.[41] To reverse this cosmic misfortune, Unificationism places great emphasis on the moral and spiritual development of its members, emphasizing they are to become selfless lovers of the divine before assuming conjugal rights and responsibilities. Despite strict premarital and extra-marital prohibitions, Rev. Moon exalts the value—indeed spiritual value— of a satisfying sexual relationship between the married couple.[42]

A former President of the American Unification Church, W. Farley Jones states that preparation for marriage should focus on the character and attitude of the individual marriage partners:

"A lifestyle of discipline and service is intended to mature one's ability to give, to serve and to truly love, thereby allowing each person to realize his true human character. The spiritual, psychological and emotional maturity of each partner is the first requirement for a successful union."[43] Jones emphasizes that before marrying "partners are to remain pure and chaste, focusing their energy on spiritual growth and on becoming a true son or daughter to God."[44] Jones explains that the "achievement of 'true love' in marriage and building a family of such love is the central spiritual goal of one's life on earth."[45] Moon teaches that marriage has a transcendent dimension: "The most significant aspect of the blessing (in marriage) is not that you are going to gain a husband or wife; you will gain God and the universe."[46]

In *Raising Children of Peace,* a volume of essays written by American members of the Unification Church whose marriages were blessed by the Rev. Moon, the influence of their spiritual leader's teachings is apparent.[47] An author of one of the essays avers: "It may not be popular or common to state that true love comes from God and that true love was created to continue for eternity in the spiritual world—but these points certainly aren't negative factors when one examines the prospects of marriage."[48] The same author professes "the knowledge that we marry 'for eternity' creates a tremendous change in our perspective about our relationship with our spouse. The subsequent commitment to stay married for eternity helps one develop long-range patience when difficulties in the relationship arise."[49] Such idealism is balanced by a vigorous Unification belief in Original Sin and the human fallen nature: "Why do married couples struggle so much, even though they may have loved each other deeply in the beginning? We are waylaid by our own selfish, corrupted natures, and by our own wretchedly inadequate capacity to love others."[50]

It is indeed the Unification recognition of human sinfulness that underlies the messianic emphasis in this movement. God has sent a messianic redeemer figure in the person of Sun Myung Moon, whose task is to restore a bride and create the true family. In turn, the "True Parents"[51] will bless the families of all humanity to establish the kingdom of heaven on earth. Unificationists believe that as a result of Sun Myung Moon's marriage to Hak Ja Han in March 1960, a new era of the "Completed Testament Age" has been inaugurated in human history.[52] For Unificationists, Rev. and Mrs. Moon stand in the position of new Adam and new Eve, and their marriage fulfills the marriage Blessing originally intended for an unfallen Adam and Eve.

In addition to Rev. Moon's moral and spiritual teachings, Unificationists gain added strength to enter into and sustain their marriages through sharing the movement's wider religious and social vision. One of the more sensationalized features of Unification marriage ceremonies is that they are often public events in which large numbers of couples simultaneously exchange wedding vows. Soon after their own "Blessing" (wedding), the Rev. and Mrs. Moon initiated and officiated at the first of what was to be a continuing series of "mass marriages."[53] Each successive marriage has seen an increase in the number of participating couples. Rev. Moon provides a rationale for such mass marriages that refers back to the first Adamic family and the mission of Jesus, whom he believes was sent to restore Adam's family:

> If the Blessing event had happened in the Garden of Eden, it would have been the big cosmic event. However, due to the human ancestor's fall, in order to indemnify the failure to accomplish the heavenly standard in the Garden of Eden, we are holding the mass wedding ceremony.[54]

Rev. Moon has in fact given a two-fold dispensational explanation to the mass wedding ceremonies, pointing backwards to a primordial history that needs to be restored (the Fall in the Garden) and forward to the present Kingdom-building of the current participants.

Over the past thirty years, successive Blessings (mass marriages) of 430, 777, 1800, 2000, 6000, and 30,000 as well as 360,000 couples were presided over by Rev. and Mrs. Moon. Up through the 430 Couples Blessing in 1968, the participants in these mass weddings were exclusively Korean.[55] The 430 Couples Blessing was understood as a national level condition of purification for Korea, whose legendary history is said to be 4300 years long. The 777 couples mass wedding, performed in 1970, involved couples from several Eastern as well as Western nations and was explicitly conceived of as marking the moment when the Blessing was made available to all humankind. Indeed, in this as well as all later marriages, there was a significant emphasis on international and interracial marriages. Such unions are understood by Rev. and Mrs. Moon as an important condition for unifying the world community.[56] The 1975 1800 Couples Blessing, in which a significant number of Americans participated, expanded the Unificationists' mission outreach worldwide. Each Blessing group (36, 72, 120, 430, etc.) has, of course, a shared experience of one of life's defining moments and an ongoing sense of common purpose. This experience typically results in the formation of Blessing Associations that not only provide spiritual support for individual couples in need but also support for shared providential missions. This support often allows individuals and families to transcend private concern and lead a life of contribution to the public welfare, a central emphasis in Unification spirituality.

In Unificationism, marriage is the central sacrament and encompasses both a personal spiritual dimension as well as a universal providential significance. The Blessing (marriage) in Unificationism is understood as reversing the primordial fall of the first human ancestors and creating a new history of families united in a spiritual and social quest to transform and elevate world society. For Unificationists, the Blessing has profound personal meaning but also offers to marriage and family a sense of historical and global significance.

London School of Economics sociologist Eileen Barker has made an in-depth study of the social characteristics of British Unificationists, or "Moonies." Some of her conclusions are striking in their contradiction of the near ubiquitous stereotype of this new religious movement. She notes a lower percentage of abnormality among Unificationists than the control group of students.[57] Barker found members of the church to be better educated than the general British population.[58] Similarly, George Chryssides comments on the "remarkably high proportion of graduates who convert to Unificationism" and further that "one has to be fairly intelligent in order to understand [Unification teachings] in the first place."[59] Barker found that the Unification Church is unlikely to attract those who are "uninterested in religion and/or social issues."[60] The potential recruit, Barker says, is a "doer" and seeks a "practical way of improving the world, while at the same time being less interested by political or revolutionary change than many of his peers."[61]

Most interesting for our purposes are Barker's findings relating to the family backgrounds of Unificationists who, as she points out, tend not to come from poor or unhappy homes. Barker concludes that one of the reasons for joining Unificationism is the prior happy family experiences of members: "so far as Moonies are looking for warmth and affection of a secure family, this is unlikely to be because they have never known one, they are far more likely to be hoping to return to one."[62]

As indicated earlier, a great majority of early Unificationists in the United States lived communally. In 1982, however, a significant percentage of this core membership changed their marital status from single to married; accordingly the structure of the Unification movement was to change. For most members, communal living became a memory and a home-based, family movement replaced it.[63] Thus, the mid 1980s saw a re-orientation of the Unification Church "towards a more denominational form of organization on the local level."[64] In sociological terms, in the 1980s, the Unification movement became a more flexible and less unitary kind of organization. It also became more capable of broader influence. Most notably, the movement made a massive investment—estimated at well over one billion dollars—in the *Washington Times* beginning in the early 1980s. By the 90s, the *Times* had become a significant voice in national politics and was a leader in the "family values" debate. Few would doubt that the benefactor's concerns did not influence the *Washington Times* singular focus on the issue.[65]

Whatever the controversy swirling in Rev. Moon's background,[66] he appears even in his 80s (he was born in 1920) to continue to expand his work. Indeed, the evolution of Unification marriage and family practices may have undergone increased acceleration over the past several years. Since 1992, the overwhelming majority of the gigantic numbers of couples participating in the Rev. Moon's Blessing ceremonies had been previously married and were not members of his church. For these non-Unificationist couples, participation in the Blessing ceremony appears to be an opportunity to re-dedicate their marriages to God as well as an affirmation of their commitment to the Unification ideal of eternal true love.

Within the Unification restoration perspective, there is an emphasis on the initial spiritual centrality of the woman/wife. In order to reverse the original fallen family of Adam and Eve, all Unification wives stand in an objective relationship to the true Father, who represents the restored Adam. As a result, the wife, during the first three years of Unification marriage, is considered the spiritual center of her own family. The husband is exhorted to unite with the heartistic or spiritual orientation of the wife and to grow into the restored Adam's position, or the true husband/father. The initial subordinate spiritual status of the husband in the marriage relationship is, however, temporary and transitional. Only with God as their center can the husband and wife achieve true unity. In the words of Rev. Moon, "Speaking from a man's position, there is no love without a woman. And a woman would say love is not possible without a man. But this is a reciprocal relationship that cannot by itself be an absolute standard of love. Without God, a reciprocal relationship cannot be ideal."[67] This concept of theocentric marriage is expressed dramatically and concretely in multitudinous sermons of Rev. Moon.

Rev. Moon sermonizes often on the genuine ideal relationship which husbands and wives should achieve. He goes so far as to admonish his followers to consider their sexual organ as belonging to their spouse: "Actually the owner of man's sexual organ is woman, and the owner of woman's sexual organ is man....Everyone is mistaken concerning ownership of the sexual organs."[68] In this spirit, the husband and wife are to understand their own sexual organ and urges as intended for the fulfillment of the other's happiness. Moreover, spouses should develop a consciousness which comprehends such urges as reflecting the divine desire to express love to their spouse: "You must put everything into God's hands. If you enter a marriage, you must be able to make love with God at the center."[69]

The Unification faith offers not only teachings on family life, but also religious practices, to help internalize these teachings. Unificationists are recommended to read at home with the entire family from fifteen volumes of Rev. Moon's selected sermons chosen for this purpose.[70] These volumes are intended to provide families with spiritual guidance directed toward familial spiritual advancement. Unification families also hold a weekly home religious service at 5:00 A.M. every Sunday as well as at 7:00 A.M. on their several holidays. The home ceremony is called the Family Pledge service and consists of recitation in unison by all present of eight pledges which express the Unificationist's commitment to God, family, nation and world. The recitation is followed by a prayer normally offered by the father and then silent or unison prayer by the entire family. At the end of the service, husband and wife typically bow to each other, and may kiss each or hug each other thereafter. Next, children bow before their parents and then parents and children exchange kisses and embrace. If grandparents are present, then all members of the family (including parents and children) will bow to the grandparents. Some families will also end with a brief spiritual reading from the teachings of Rev. Moon or the Bible.

The outward ceremonial dimensions of this Unification family service certainly reflect Korean and Confucian social teachings and customs. Yet the content of the teachings owe far more to traditional Christian views of grace and gratitude to God. Parents as well as children are advised to be grateful for each other because through the parent-child relationship, they can experience the love of God on Earth. Unificationists remind themselves through the weekly pledge service that their familial, social and religious responsibilities define their purpose on the earth: "Our family pledges…centered on true love…to become individuals of filial piety for the family, patriots to the nation, saints for the world, and holy sons and daughters of Heaven and Earth."[71]

It is well known that Rev. Moon has served as a matchmaker for many of the couples he has blessed. Currently, sheer numbers, along with the fact of Rev. Moon's advancing age, suggests a new practice may be emerging with respect to the engagement of couples. Given the Confucian influences in the background of Unificationism, it may be that parents will become more directly involved in the selection of their children's marriage partners than has become the case in Western modernity.[72] Unificationism is at this point a first-generation movement, and no doubt much of its future will lie with its founding members' children-the second generation. Unificationists understand their children to be born without original sin and as thus possessing an enhanced potential for spiritual development.[73] This viewpoint may in part explain the heightened sensitivity evident in Unification child-rearing practices, which emphasize a pure lifestyle and instilling a sense of personal responsibility within the context of a loving family.

In closing, an American Unificationist's description of his manner after disciplining his son may reflect something of the family spirit of this movement that has proved appealing to so many:

> They (our children) need our forgiveness, our faith, and our belief in them. When my son, Ranin, apologizes, I go to him and kiss his cheek, and say, 'That's all right, Ranin. Thank you for saying sorry.' I then follow up by expressing warmth to him for the next few moments, reestablishing the conviction in his mind that his daddy loves him and thinks that he is the most wonderful Ranin in the whole world.[74]

THE PROMISE KEEPERS: COACHING MEN TO BE CHAMPION HUSBANDS

On March 20, 1990, Bill McCartney first verbalized his dream to a friend: "I envision men coming together in high numbers worshipping and celebrating their faith together. I long to see men openly proclaiming their love for Christ and their commitment to their families."[75] Soon afterwards, McCartney, a born-again Christian and head football coach at the University of Colorado, gathered together seventy men who agreed to pray about "mobilizing men around a spiritual focus rather than politics, sports, or career interests."[76] In July 1991, more than 4,200 men attended the first conference in Boulder, Colorado.[77] "And that was only the beginning of the vision for the Promise Keepers,"[78] McCartney thereafter said. McCartney's hope is to fill stadiums in every state at the same time. In 1996, he gathered more than one million men in 22 cities across America and in a single event on October 4, 1997, the Promise Keepers brought hundreds of thousands of men to the Mall in Washington, D.C.

Although not without its setbacks, the Promise Keepers undoubtedly was one of the the most significant American religious phenomenon of the 90s. The Promise Keepers addresses directly the decline of male spirituality and sense of family responsibility: "I believe we've sat idle too long in this country as men abdicated the role of leadership to their wives. Men have drifted away from God and their wives. And they've turned a deaf ear when their children needed them."[79]

Who are the men attending the Promise Keepers rallies and why do they come? John Spaulding tells us that the median age of Promise Keepers attendees is 38.[80] Although 88 percent are married, 21 percent have been divorced and only 25 percent are satisfied with themselves as fathers. The demographics of attendees at the 1997 and 1998 rallies do reflect change, but the majority of the participants are still white.[81] Most telling is Ken Abraham's observation upon attending one such rally in Pittsburgh: "Guys who ordinarily struggled to stay awake during their pastor's brief sermon back home listened enthusiastically to one speaker after another throughout the day."[82] Their responsiveness may have something to do with a message "steeped in sports imagery" and frequently relating being a better husband, father and citizen "to winning the big game or competing in the heat of battle."[83] Nevertheless, most observers, as well as participants and their spouses, agree that many have had a profound religious experience, which has a continuing impact on their lives."[84] Many of the men are both responding to the call of a spiritual awakening as well as seeking the power to become more faithful, committed husbands and responsible fathers: "Promise Keepers fortifies the hope in men that they can stand against what many perceive as the sliding sludge caused by the erosion of values in society."[85]

Beyond the religious fervor of Promise Keepers' conferences, men are encouraged to keep seven promises. The founding members of Promise Keepers were convinced that many societal ills are caused by broken promises—from marriage vows to business and community commitments.[86] On the individual level, Promise Keepers stresses marital fidelity, encouraging men to practice moral and sexual purity. McCartney reports that 62 percent of Promise Keepers surveyed struggle with sexual immorality—"the spectrum of lust, pornography, adultery, fornication, and homosexuality."[87] The Promise Keepers enjoins men to abstain from all sexual relations except that between husband and wife. Participants are aware that this demand cuts against the grain of the dominant culture. A twenty-two year old unmarried college student who converted to Christianity at a Promise Keepers conference expressed his surprise that the Bible forbids pre-marital sex: "I have grown up with television and the movies, where if a guy and a woman care for each other, sex is a natural part of their relationship...I never dreamed in my wildest imagination that God had anything to say about sex."[88] Recognizing the challenge presented by Promise three on sexual purity, Promise Keepers encourages men to establish relationships with God (Promise one) and a small group of male friends (Promise two). These first two promises are to provide the spiritual basis for fulfilling Promise three as well as the remaining four Promises which focus on social responsibilities. Many Promise Keepers become born-again Christians upon attending their first conference. They, as well as all other attendees, are encouraged to continue praying daily and to build an unbreakable bond of trust with Jesus. This vertical relationship is essential but, Promise Keepers would allow, not sufficient. On the horizontal level, Promise Keepers are instructed to develop at least a few close male friendships. Indeed, the small groups which Promise Keepers form are first and foremost prayer groups. Many men learn to share their hearts openly for the first time at a Promise Keepers rally. It is such transparency in the relationships among a small group of men that Promise Keepers say is vital to maintaining personal support and accountability to be faithful husbands, fathers and citizens. According to the Promise Keepers, such accountability requires the willingness of a man "to submit his life to a group or at least one other individual, to whom he grants the right to inspect key personal and professional matters."[89]

A primary purpose of such male bonding for Promise Keepers is to help men to fulfill Promise number four: to love wife and children. The Promise Keepers view men in their home as having withdrawn and failing to meet their God-given responsibilities as husbands and fathers. As McCartney sees it: "There can be little doubt that God has used Promise Keepers to help redefine the term masculinity—a man's man is a Godly man—and foster a long overdue role reversal among the sexes, whereby men are now beginning to assume greater responsibility for spiritual and servant-hearted leadership in the home."[90]

The emphasis on men leading in the home has elicited harsh criticism from some quarters. For instance, *NOW*, the National Organization of Women, has criticized the Promise Keepers as seeking to revive the patriarchal household and as fundamentally misogynistic.[91] Yet the vast majority of Promise Keepers' wives acknowledge that their husbands have been changed for the better—listening to them, helping in the household with chores and the children with homework, etc.[92]

Two aspects of Promise Keepers' central teaching are challenging: the unfamiliarity and seemingly contradictory concept of servant-leadership and the assertion of responsible male authority within the household. The staged washing of women's feet by their husbands at Promise Keepers rallies suggests more than a revival of patriarchalism as the goal. Robert Wuthnow of Princeton's Center for the Study of American Religion has remarked, "Contrary to what some critics say—that Promise Keepers is turning them into real macho men—its domesticating them."[93]

Certainly part of this domestication is related to the fifth Promise which men are asked to keep, namely to support their local church. Clearly one of the transformations in many men attending a Promise Keepers rally is a renewed or new involvement in their local churches upon returning home. A Lutheran pastor of a Houston church has remarked on the Promise Keep-

ers' prominent role in renewing churches: "so often in American
culture, religion is considered women's work."[94] Here again,
Promise Keepers seems at the end of the century to be challenging a prevailing twentieth-century notion of masculinity. Although some church leaders have expressed worry that the men's
enthusiasm for Promise Keepers might result in less charitable
giving directed to them, the Promise Keepers make a point of
instructing its membership that they should tithe to their local
church before making any donations to it. At Promise Keepers
conferences, all attending ministers are treated to thunderous
applause and expressions of appreciation from rally speakers.
Writing in *Christian Century*, one minister of a mainline denomination eulogizes the Promise Keepers: "This sensitivity to
and elevation of the ministry is without parallel in my seminary
and congregational experience."[95]

The Promise Keepers aspires to transcend racial and denominational prejudices, constituting the sixth Promise which they
are committed to keeping. Bill McCartney appears to be deeply
committed to both aspects of this Promise despite considerable
criticism of them from within the Christian community. Fundamentalists oppose Promise Keepers' openness to charismatic
Christians and Roman Catholics.[96] However, Promise Keepers'
officials state they prefer to emphasize similarities rather than
dwell on differences within Christianity. McCartney succeeded
in bringing together over 39,000 ministers at one of his conferences in the fall of 1996—the largest gathering ever of interde-
nominational Christian ministers.[97] The Promise Keepers
presented more or less their normal call for renewal of commitment to God and family, as well as to interracial and interde-
nominational cooperation. One Presbyterian nevertheless
reported on his own as well as his fellow ministers' response:

"Although they quibbled with some elements of the event, they found the overall experience deeply compelling ."[98] He tells of the attentive silence in the stadium as a speaker spoke "with devastating accuracy [of] the impact that church careers have on spouses and children"[99] and of the many who could be heard weeping.

According to Promise Keepers' surveys, 37 percent of pastors have confessed to being inappropriately involved in sexual behavior with someone in the church, and nearly 50 percent have admitted to experiencing sexual problems in their marriages.[100] Thus, the Promise Keepers have reason to believe that their basic message has relevance for the clergy of the land. No doubt, McCartney saw added significance in this clergy conference, for in attendance were the potential barrier-breakers of the denominational walls dividing Christianity.

McCartney has consistently and loudly decried racism, which he understands to be a major stain upon the church: "...the ten o'clock hour on Sunday is the country's most segregated hour of the week."[101] McCartney's stand against racism predates his involvement with the Promise Keepers. He was the only head coach of a Division I-A collegiate football team to have an equal number of men of color and Caucasians on his coaching staff.[102] However, there is little question that both his sensitivity and commitment to the race issue was dramatically heightened beginning with the first Boulder conference in 1991. He recounts an epiphanic moment: "towards the end of that program, as I casually gazed in amazement on the crowd, my eye caught something. It sent a chill down my spine; the crowd was almost entirely white."[103] Then he went on to proclaim that although they could anticipate a sellout gathering next year, God would not join them unless "a fair representation of all God's people" were present.[104] McCartney's remarks on racism were responded to by a barrage of hate mail and chastising "corrections" of his errant scriptural understanding. McCartney did gain additional insight from this reaction: "...a first glimpse of the seething giant of racism lurking within the fabric of the Christian church."[105]

McCartney has never backed off his position against racism despite the continuing criticism and cost. Following the 1991 conference, McCartney went to several major cities to speak on the issue of race. He recalls the thunderous applause from the audience upon his introduction and then the silence following his message—"...a morgue-like chill as I stepped away from the microphone."[106] Within the setting of regular Promise Keepers conferences he fares better, but even there in 1996, 40 percent of all complaints were reactions to the reconciliation theme. The movement's choice to advocate multiracialism and to not just reinforce existing beliefs is challenging to some conference participants.[107] Some speculate that McCartney's obsession with the racial issue is his way of coping with the trauma of a daughter who gave birth to two out-of-wedlock children fathered by two men of color who were players on his football team.[108] Others criticize McCartney and his organization for not addressing the social dimensions of racism—equality of jobs, housing and education, etc. Both criticisms ignore the deeply religious character of the man and his movement. McCartney believes/feels that he has experienced God's heart on the matter of race and it is this divine will which he seeks to realize.[109] He continued to cry out that "by the year 2000, racism within the church will have been eradicated."[110]

No doubt the spectacular growth of the Promise Keepers during its brief lifetime inspires visions of much greater deeds to be accomplished in the near future. In October 1997, the Promise Keepers gathered hundreds of thousands of Christian men in Washington, D.C. on the National Mall, ranking in number with the largest events ever held there.[111]

Still, the path taken has not been without obstacles and disappointment for McCartney and his organization. In 1997 and 1998, attendance at rallies was below expectations. The organization contemplated in February 1998 laying off its entire staff and relying on volunteers. In October 1998, Promise Keepers decided to reduce its full-time staff by 28 percent, from 250 to 180.[112]

Promise Keepers' financial difficulty was largely self-inflicted, for in the fall of 1997, McCartney had decided to eliminate the $60-$70 fee charged to conference participants and change to a donation-based operation. The intended result from this change has already been achieved, namely a significant increase of ethnically diverse participants as well as non-Christian men. More recent first time attendees also have lower incomes and are slightly younger than in the past.[113] Income from resource sales and month-to-month gifts remain substantial. Nevertheless, the Promise Keepers' plan for an immense turn of the millennium gathering of families at state capitals across the nation was not realized.[114] The movement, however, continues to bring together men in conferences throughout the nation. After all, the seventh and last Promise of the Promise Keepers is to "encourage other men to do likewise."[115]

McCartney's effectiveness as a positive role model and his capacity to inspire tens of thousands of American men to be better husbands and fathers may have as much to do with his weaknesses as his virtues. Certainly, his sensational success as head coach of the University of Colorado football team gave him a profile which many American males admire. His wife,

Lyndi McCartney, has said of him: "I also believe God chose Bill because he is a product of our American culture and therefore can be an example of common mistakes men in our culture make with regard to their wives and children."[116] McCartney admits to a long battle with alcoholism that took him years to overcome. Further, he admits to having "sold out" to a culture of success wherein in his quest for professional excellence he almost totally ignored his wife and children.[117] McCartney, as well as other Promise Keepers, speakers do not hide their failings from conference attendees. McCartney has also confessed that even his "hard-charging approach" to his Promise Keepers ministry prevented him from fulfilling his role as husband and father.[118] This transparency in McCartney's presentations is most effective in helping to transform other conference attendees. Fortified by his God, McCartney's willingness to beg forgiveness from his wife and children and to become a devoted husband and father may show a way back home for many American men.

Conclusion

Religion and Family in the Twenty-First Century

SUMMARY

In the Introduction, the social-scientific evidence is reviewed demonstrating the decisive and positive role which religion plays in American families in the present time. Religion helps families not only to remain intact, but also to prosper and attain higher levels of happiness even when cultural, social and economic conditions inimical to family life pertain. This efficacious impact of religion on family life is contrasted to the failed attempts of politicians and legislators to strengthen American families.

The body of the work examines the historical role of Christianity in shaping the expectations and practices of the Western family. It is shown that Christianity has a distinguished record of promoting family values arising from its founder's unique teachings, even against hostile cultural traditions. The inherent limitations of public policy to bolster the family are reflected in Chapter One's opening review of Emperor Augustus' unsuccessful interventions to improve the Roman family. Chapter One examines the distinctive marital teachings of Jesus, the command to life-long monogamous marriage in the context of first-century Mediterranean family life. Fortified by the words of Jesus on marriage, Christian leaders often made heroic efforts in opposition to aristocratic and royal spousal abuse of women. In the later Middle Ages, the church succeeded in sacralizing marriage and establishing life-long monogamy as normative. Further, the Christian ethic fostered a culture supportive both directly and indirectly of families and children. In the fourth and fifth centuries, for instance, wealthy widowed women were encouraged to forsake a second marriage and to devote their resources to serve destitute children and women.

In Chapter Two, the central role of Protestant Christianity in fostering companionate marriage is documented. Protestantism acknowledged the marital state as normative for Christian life: ministers were not merely allowed to marry, but married life was seen as a prerequisite for successful ministry. The home was reconceived as a private church where family members constituted the community of believers loving each other as Christ loved. The formative influence on the American national psyche of the Puritan emphasis on family life is described, as is Puritanism's concomitant skepticism regarding the role of government. Nineteenth-century American Christianity contributed significantly to the feminization of family life, affirming the moral and spiritual authority of women in the household. The decline of men in their participation in churches as well as from being significant players in family life accelerated in the twentieth century.

In Chapter Three, Christianity's enormous influence in elevating the status of children as spiritual equals to adults is explained. Once again, the words of the founder of Christianity initiate and sustain the reform efforts of the church in enhancing the respect for children in the West. The progressive efforts of the ancient church, medieval Catholicism, and finally modern Christianity both in combating the exploitation of children and in achieving an affective appreciation of children are reviewed.

Central to Christian, and perhaps all religious child-rearing approaches, is the emphasis on the self-discipline of the parents. Parents are encouraged to control their emotions so as to act in the best interests of the child. Ironically, it was the Enlightenment and secular child-rearing theories that emphasized achieving control over the child so as to mold the child in accord with socially constructed ideals of normalcy. The precariousness of the contemporary child's new status, dependent upon the emotional satisfaction of parents without religious commitment, is also noted.

In Chapter Four, the efforts of the two largest American Christian denominations to sustain marriages and prepare youth and engaged couples for successful married life are examined throughout the last half of the twentieth century. The Southern Baptist Convention (SBC) and the Roman Catholic Church account for more than one-third of all American Christians, and their family ministries have been steadily intensifying spiritually, theologically and professionally over the past several decades. Wracked by extraordinary tensions over a range of sexual issues, Roman Catholics, nonetheless, have consistently generated, over the past fifty years programs to strengthen families from the Cana Conference and Catholic Family Movement to Marriage Encounter, Retrouvaille and, most recently, Catholic Familyland. Troubled by the broader culture which it considered inhospitable to Christian family values, the SBC has mounted a massive counter-cultural youth movement, "True Love Waits" as well as developed an alternative entertainment industry producing twenty-four-hour family programs for radio and television. The SBC has also provided extensive and sophisticated Internet sites offering help to all members of the family for virtually every problem, practical as well as spiritual. Many of the endeavors by

Roman Catholics and the SBC have been adopted or adapted widely by other Christian denominations in America and abroad.

In Chapter Five, the contribution of three new religious movements to the well-being of the American family in the twentieth century is examined. Mormonism, Unificationism and the Promise Keepers are responding to the increasing materialistic focus and declining spirituality of the American family, as well as the virtual disappearance of the father's role within the contemporary family. These movements further testify to the continuing, although protean, power of Christianity in shaping family life at the end of the twentieth century.

In putting forth the thesis that Christianity has had historically and continues to have significant impact on the family in the West, one cannot and should not entirely dismiss certain negative consequences of this influence. While the feminization of Church and family reversed inveterate patterns of oppression of women in these institutions and allowed for a greater valuation and concern for the most vulnerable members of the family, namely children, it also led to an unhealthy diminished sense of responsibility and role for husbands and fathers in the modern family. I would argue that Christianity itself contains the spiritual resources to redress this imbalance and to support fathers and husbands to assume greater responsibility and authority within the family. But this cannot be a call backwards to a time when women were deemed inferior and treated as of lesser value than men. It is, rather, a step towards an ideal of marriage as a new partnership in which both commit themselves to loving the other in Christ. Such mutual love will sustain them in fulfilling their responsibility as spouses and parents. The historical consequences of Christianity and of other religions cannot be judged apart from the concrete social circumstances that they encounter and seek to transform. There are moral absolutes and ideals, but they can only be progressively realized over time. Christianity's impact on the Western family is best understood as a trajectory towards an ideal of marriage as a divinely ordained spiritual and physical union.

Despite recent public attention to horrendous instances of the sexual abuse of children perpetrated by a minority of Catholic clerics, I have argued in this work that historically celibacy has functioned in Catholic Christianity as a means to sustain families and especially children in need. In this sense, paradoxically, celibate men and women came to the aid of families in times of distress when child abandonment and its tragic consequences abounded. Such conditions defined most of Western history and still persist in many parts of the world today. Given the particularly vitriolic past polemics between Protestants and Catholics over the relative spiritual status of celibates versus marrieds, the recognition that religious celibates have so often served to strengthen families may be salutary. It is clear that any reconsideration of the requirement of clerical celibacy would need to take place within the context of the ample historical, theological and spiritual resources of the Catholic tradition.

CONCLUSION: WHERE DO WE GO FROM HERE?

It has been the argument of this work that the churches historically, and also at present, have been a singularly significant factor in family well-being. Given the acknowledged causal relationship between disrupted and single parent families and a host of social ills, from poverty and crime to school drop-out rates and suicide, the recognition of the power of religion to support the family is of paramount importance. Faith-based families and family-based religion are a fundamental requirement for the spiritual rejuvenation of Western society in the twenty-first century. In the latter part of the twentieth century, a mass culture of materialism and self-centered individualism has called into question the gains that have been made for families in the Christian West.

Government has rightly come to recognize the limits of its efficacy in dealing with social and particularly family problems and has turned to private philanthropy and especially the churches to assume a greater share of the social burden. The recent government decision not to discriminate against faith-based social welfare programs even when conducted by churches, but to support the programs based on their effectiveness in helping the needy as measured by their outcomes, is expressive of the government's realization of the limitations of the welfare state.

Yet at this same time, respected leaders of mainline Christian denominations often seem confused about, or unwilling to, reaffirm traditional teachings on sexuality, marriage and divorce. In his November, 1997 homily celebrating the fiftieth wedding anniversary of Queen Elizabeth II, the Archbishop of Canterbury reportedly "went out of his way to avoid slighting" members of the royal family with broken marriages.[1] Three of the four children of Queen Elizabeth have been divorced and the fourth has until recently been unmarried. No commentary has so far remarked on the oddity of an English Archbishop publicly and pointedly absolving and comforting divorcing royals as simply less fortunate than those experiencing a "long-lasting" marriage. Rather, with a few notable exceptions, Christian leaders have historically been courageous in rebuking the kind of extra-marital escapades which brought Diana to despair of her union with Charles. As we have seen, the ideal of life-long monogamous marriage was not ready-made in the West, but was a standard which Christianity battled for centuries to establish. Before Christianity and the West inadvertently or capriciously abandon this family norm, we should make ourselves aware of the historical struggle which has made it possible.

Given the now widely recognized importance of families to societal well-being, it is critical at this time that Christianity reaffirm its historical commitment to life-long monogamy and to the responsibility of parents to their children as well as children to their parents. In light of the Herculean efforts—described throughout this book—that the Christian church has expended to establish those commitments in society, it would be foolhardy for the churches to let these achievements slip away now. Ecclesiastical leaders worried about opposing a social trend should take heart from the fact that for most of its history, the church's position on such issues was contrary to the mainstream culture. The increasing demand by the laity for an explicitly spiritual approach, especially with respect to family ministries in the late 1980s and 1990s, suggests that church leaders may be pleasantly surprised by the response of their members. Moreover, the fact is that liberal, mainline denominations that have either compromised or been ambiguous about traditional Christian family values have suffered substantial membership declines over the last several decades. Whereas evangelical and other conservative churches emphasizing Christian nurturing of families have been thriving during this same period.[2]

A primary commitment of churches should be to promote faith-based families and to measure their success by the spiritual strength of such families. An important standard of a pastor's competence should be his/her ability to empower heads of households as spiritual leaders of their families. Spiritual leadership should be shared between husband and wife; children, as they grow older, should also have increasing responsibility to provide spiritual nourishment to other members of the family. The church should be developing home rituals that help family members recognize and nurture the spiritual dimension of their household relationships. In this regard, Christianity may have much to learn from Judaism, wherein a number of important religious rituals are family-centered. Some dormant Christian traditions, such as saying grace at meals and family prayer meetings with readings from the Bible or other religious material and discussion, should be revitalized. Churches should encourage their members to undertake such practices; they should also hold family workshops and provide opportunities for faith-based families to share their testimonies with others. Faith-based families are the strength of the church and the church should support them.

Neither the state nor the Church nor the schoolhouse can fulfill the conjugal, parental and filial responsibilities incumbent on family members. And not even a village can substitute for the personal and direct care of the father and mother in raising a child. Yet fathers are conspicuously absent in the American family today. In the nineteenth century, American men moved out into the work place and abandoned the places where the human character and spirit are forged—the home, the house of worship as well as the schools. Men became gradually cut off from meaningful involvement with their own families, displaced by the "angel in the home."[3]

Concurrent with the decline of family commitment and the despiritualization of American men, there arose opportunities for unprecedented material satisfaction for even the average American household. The relative material abundance of American families took place within the wider context of a consumerist culture driven by the now omnipresent electronic mass media, accelerating the secularization of family culture. As increasing numbers of mothers entered the work force, an immense void was felt in the home, which was in large part filled by daycare centers and an ever ready electronic nanny: TV. Although a few advocate a return to a simpler, pre-modern lifestyle and, thus, isolation from the wider culture, a more promising alternative is for wives/mothers and especially husbands/fathers together to assume responsibility for nurturing the spiritual life of their families. Effective family ministries will, for instance, provide the context and encouragement for parents to think through the trade-off between earning the means to greater comfort and luxury and the availability of quality time to spend together as a family. Parents and maturing children should discuss such issues openly and patiently, and develop options that satisfy their spiritual as well as material needs. Christian leaders should serve to facilitate such mini-church or family dialogues throughout their congregations.

Given that the wider cultural, economic and government influences are often effectively hostile to the family in modern America, the unique role that religion may play in support of families is even more important. Individuals who actively nurture their spiritual life are better able to sustain and enjoy marriage and family life. Religion in the twenty-first century should become family centered, oriented toward strengthening the spiritual well-being of families. Faith-based families and family-based religion are the necessary and achievable cornerstone of a peaceful, abundant and progressive new millennium for all humankind.

NOTES

INTRODUCTION:

1 See Darwin L. Thomas and Gwendolyn C. Henry, "The Religion and Family Connection: Increasing Dialogue in the Social Sciences," in *Journal of Marriage and Family*, May 1985, vol. 47, no. 2, pp. 369-379.

2 Former President Jimmy Carter, in a 1996 interview, said in reference to difficulties in his marriage in its initial years: "These conflicts would have been serious enough to threaten our marriage were it not for the sustaining religious faith we shared." Herbert Wray, "A Georgia Farmer Takes Stock" in *U.S. News & World Report*, December 9, 1996; p. 86.

3 Sar A. Levitan and Richard S. Belous, *What's Happening to the American Family?*, (Baltimore, The Johns Hopkins University, 1981), p. VII.

4 In 1960, the percentage was 53 percent, see *U.S. News & World Report*, "The Decline of the Two-Parent Family"; Feb. 19,1996; p. 22.

5 Eric Schmitt; "Nuclear Families Drop Below 25% of Households for First Time"; May 15, 2001; *The New York Times*, p. A1.

6 *Statistical Abstract of the United States 1995 (115th edition)*; U.S. Department of Commerce, Economics and Statistics Administration; Bureau of the Census; p. 61.

7 See "Poll Reveals More Acceptance of a Changing American Family"; November, 29, 1999; *The New York Times*, p. A41.

8 *Statistical Abstract*, p. 61.

9 Ibid.

10 Elaine Tyler May, "Myths and Realities of the American Family" in *A History of Private Life: Riddles of Identity in Modern Times*, Antoine Prost and Gerard Vincente eds., (Harvard University Press, 1991), pp. 590-1.

11 See R. W. Apple for "His Battle Now Lost, Moynihan Still Cries Out," Fri., August, 2, 1996, *The New York Times*, p. A16.

12 Ibid.

13 Sara S. McLanahan, "The Consequences of Single Motherhood," *in The American Prospect*, Summer 1994, pp. 48-58; quote from p. 49.

14 Peter W. Greenwood, "Juvenile Crime and Juvenile Justice," p. 96 in James Q. Wilson and Joan Petersilia ed., *Crime*, (San Francisco, ICS Press, 1995), pp. 91-117.

15 Ibid., p. 104.

16 Ibid., p. 91.

17 Travis Hirschi, "The Family," p. 136 in James Q. Wilson and Joan Petersilia ed., *Crime*, (San Francisco, ICS Press, 1995), pp. 121-140.

18 Robert J. Sampson, "The Community," p. 198 in James Q. Wilson and Joan Petersilia ed., *Crime*, (San Francisco, ICS Press, 1995), pp. 193-216.

19 *Statistical Abstract*, p. 66, no. 70.

20 Ibid., p. 103, no. 146.

21 Levitan and Belous, *American Family*, p. 58.

22 Judith S. Wallerstein and Sandra Blakeslee, *Second Chances: Men, Women, and Children A Decade After Divorce*, (NY, Ticknor & Fields, 1989), p. X.

23 Ibid., XV.

24 Ibid., XVII.

25 Ibid., 303.

26 McLanahan, "The Consequences," p. 51.

27 See Donald T. Critchlow, *Intended Consequences: Birth Control, Abortion and the Federal Government in Modern America*, NY: Oxford University, 1999, pp. 10-11, passim.

28 See Steven A. Holmes; "Birth Rate Falls to 40-Year Low Among Unwed Black Women"; *NY Times*; July 1, 1998; p. A1.

29 Ibid., p. A16.

30 The Consortium of State Physicians Resource Councils noted a steep decline in the use of oral contraceptives between 1988 and 1995, offsetting increased use of condoms and resulting in a total decrease of contraceptive use among teenagers of 14.5 percent. See Helen Alvarez; "Behind the Drop in Teen-age Births"; *NY Times*; May 4, 1999; p. A30.

31 President Clinton, however, in his first term in office expressed disagreement with the view that same-sex marriage should be accorded an equivalent legal status to that of heterosexual marriage.

32 Levitan and Belous, *American Family*, p. 188.

33 Allan Carlson, "The Family: Where Do We Go From Here?" in *Transaction: Social Science and Modern Society*, vol. 32:5; July/August 1995, p. 65.

34 Ibid.

35 Gilbert Y. Steiner, *The Futility of Family Policy*, Washington, D.C.: The Brookings Institution, 1981, p. 10.

36 Ibid., p. 215.

37 Ibid., p. 8.

38 Charles Trueheart, "Welcome to the Next Church," *The Atlantic Monthly*, August 1996, p. 40.

39 See "The Faith Factor: Can Churches Cure America's Social Ills?," Joseph P. Shapiro, *U.S. News & World Report*, Sept. 9, 1996, p. 47.

40 Freeman quoted by Robert Rector in "God and the Underclass," *National Review*, July 15, 1996, vol. 48:13, pp. 30-33.

41 Steven Stack, "The Effect of Domestic/Religious Individualism on Suicide, 1954-1978," *Journal of Marriage and Family*, 1985, vol. 47:2, pp. 431-447, p.441.

42 Thomas and Henry, "The Religion and Family Connection," p.369.

43 Ibid., p. 371.

44 Ibid., p. 376.

45 Roger Doyle, *Atlas of Contemporary America: A Portrait of the Nation*, (N.Y.: Facts On File, June, 1994), p. 20.

46 Ibid.

47 Ibid., p. 16.

48 Paul Johnson, in "God and the Americas" notes that more than half of the American people still attend worship services on any given weekend, a percentage unparalleled in any other major nation of the world. See *Commentary*, January 1995, vol. 99:1, pp. 25-45

49 See Arland Thornton, William G. Axinn, Daniel H. Hill, "Reciprocal Effects of Religiosity, Cohabitation, and Marriage" in *American Journal of Sociology*, 1992, vol. 98:3, pp. 648-9.

50 Ibid., pp. 629-650.

51 Ibid., p. 638.

52 Ibid., p. 647.

53 Ibid.

54 The researchers also posit a reciprocal effect of adolescent sexual behavior on religious participation arguing that sexually active adolescents are as a result less likely to become or remain religiously involved. See Arland Thornton and Donald Camburn, "Religious Participation and Adolescent Sexual Behavioral Attitudes" in *Journal of Marriage & the Family*, vol. 51:3, August 1989, pp. 641-653.

55 See Larry Jensen and Janet Jensen, "Family Values, Religiosity, and Gender," p. 430, in *Psychology Reports*, 1993, vol. 73, pp. 429-30.

56 It is widely known that Middletown signifies Muncie, Indiana. See Theodore Caplow et al. *Middletown Families: Fifty Years of Change and Continuity*, (Minneapolis, University of Minnesota, 1982).

57 See Howard M. Bahr and Bruce A. Chadwick, "Religion and Family in

Middletown, U.S.A." in *Journal of Marriage and Family*, May 1985, vol. 47:2, pp. 407-414.

58 Ibid., p. 411.

59 Ibid., p. 412.

60 Ibid.; p. 413.

61 Ibid.

62 Kip W. Jenkins, "Religion and Families" in *Family Research: A Sixty-Year Review, 1930-1990*, vol. 1, edited by Stephen J. Bahr, (NY: Lexington Books, 1991), pp. 235-288, particularly p. 269.

63 Erik E. Filsinger and Margaret R. Wilson, "Religiosity, Socio-economic Reward, and Family Development: Predictors of Marital Adjustment" in *Journal of Marriage and Family*, August 1984, vol. 46:3, pp. 663-670.

64 Ibid., p. 667.

65 Ibid.

66 Melvin L. Wilkinson and William C. Tanner III, "The Influence of Family Size, Interaction, and Religiosity on Family Affection in a Mormon Sample," *Journal of Marriage and Family*, 1980, vol. 42, pp. 297-304.

67 Ibid.; p. 302.

68 M. A. Johnson, "Family Life and Religious Commitment," *Review of Religious Research*, 1973, vol. 14, pp. 165-180.

69 See Edward O. Laumann, John H. Gagnon, Robert Michael, and Stuart Michaels, *The Social Organization of Sexuality: Sexual Practices in the United States*, (Chicago, The University of Chicago Press, 1994), p. 115.

70 Ibid., p. 115.

71 See Chapter 2, pp. 34-35 on the American Puritans.

CHAPTER 1:

1 See James Field, "The Purpose of the Lex Julia et Papia-Poppaea, *Classical Journal*, v. 4, (1944/45), p. 400.

2 See Paul Veyne, "The Roman Empire" ed. Aries and Duby, *A History of Private Life*, vol. 1, (Cambridge, MA; Belknap Press, 1987), pp. 35-37.

3 See Richard I. Frank, "Augustus' Legislation on Marriage and Children," in *California Studies in Classical Antiquity*, vol. 8, 1975, pp. 41-43.

4 Ibid., p. 43.

5 The official names of the three laws were: (1) *Lex Julia*, (2) *De Maritandis Ordinibus*, and (3) *Lex Papia-Poppaea*.

6 Bernard I. Murstein, *Love, Sex and Marriage Through the Ages*, (New York: Springer, 1974), p. 35.

7 Ibid., p. 43.

8 See Elizabeth Schussler-Fiorenza, *In Memory of Her*, (New York: Crossroads, 1983), p. 143.

9 Mark 1:11; It should be noted that, given the fact that Palestine is under Roman rule at this time and Roman law did allow for wives to sue for divorce, certain Jews holding Roman citizenry may have availed themselves of this right.

10 See Geoffrey Parrinder, *Sex in the World's Religions*, (New York: Oxford University, 1980), p. 202. I am grateful to Stephen Post for this reference.

11 A Hellenized city of Syria under Roman rule in Paul's time.

12 See Anthony J. Guerra, *Romans and the Apologetic Tradition: The Purpose, Genre and Meaning of Paul's Letter*, (Cambridge University, 1995).

13 Will Deming, *Paul on Marriage and Celibacy: The Hellenistic Background of I Corinthians 7*,(Cambridge: Cambridge University Press, 1995).

14 Elaine Pagels' description is most apt: "Like relatives in a large family battling over the inheritance, both ascetic and nonascetic Christians laid claim to the legacies of Jesus and Paul, both sides insisting that they alone were the true heirs." *Adam, Eve and the Serpent*, (New York: Random House, 1989), p. 25.

15 See Anthony J. Guerra, "The Conversion of Marcus Aurelius and Justin Martyr," in *The Second Century*, 9:3, 1992.

16 Veyne, "The Roman Empire," pp. 5-207.

17 See Peter Brown, "Late Antiquity," ed. Aries and Duby, *A History of Private Life*, vol. 1, (Cambridge, MA; Belknap Press, 1987), p. 251.

18 Ibid., p. 265.

19 Ibid., p. 270.

20 Note that the Christian sense of civic duty was restricted to their own community; from the perspective of the Romans, Christians could appear as lacking civic loyalties, the ostensible rationale for their persecution.

21 Brown, "Late Antiquity," p. 309.

22 See Pagels, *Adam, Eve and the Serpent*, p. 130. Pagels also notes that many early Christians also believed that they could triumph over death not only in the future resurrection, but here and now. p. 128.

23 Ibid., p. 91-95.

24 Ramsey MacMullen, *Christianizing the Roman Empire*, (New Haven: Yale, 1984), p. 86.

25 See Suzanne F. Wemple, *Women in Frankish Society: Marriage and the Cloister*, (Philadelphia: University of Pennsylvania, 1981), p. 9.

26 Ibid., pp. 24-25.

27 Ibid., pp. 33-34.

28 Ibid., p. 36.

29 Ibid., p. 158.

30 Ibid., p. 75.

31 Ibid., p. 38.

32 Ibid., p. 76.

33 Ibid., p. 77.

34 Ibid., p. 78.

35 It should be noted that the average age of women at death in this period is 36 years old.

36 Wemple, *Marriage and the Cloister*, p. 79.

37 Ibid., p. 105.

38 Georges Duby, *The Knight, the Lady and the Priest: The Making of Modern Marriage in Medieval France*, trans. Barbara Bray, (New York: Pantheon Books, 1983), p. 32.

39 Ibid., pp. 33-34.

40 Ibid., p. 48. Duby notes that ninth century inventories show peasants on large estates were firmly bonded in marriage-an arrangement benefiting, of course, the interest of their masters.

41 Ibid., pp. 67-74.

CHAPTER 2:

1 See Richard Sennett, *Families Against the City: Middle Class Homes of Industrial Chicago, 1872-1890*, (Cambridge: Harvard University Press, 1970), pp. 187-206.

2 Thomas Aquinas on *The Truth of the Catholic Faith, Book Three: Providence, Part II*, trans.; Vernon J. Bourke, (Garden City: Doubleday, 1956), p. 148; ch. 123.6.

3 Ibid., ch. 123.4.

4 Ibid., p. 152; ch. 124.4.

5 Ibid., p. 155; ch. 126.2.

6 Peter Gardella, *Innocent Ecstasy: How Christianity Gave America an Ethic of Sexual Pleasure*, (NY: Oxford University, 1985), pp. 11-12

7 Desiderius Erasmus, *The Colloquies of Erasmus*, trans. Craig R. Thompson,

(Chicago: University of Chicago, 1965), p. 95.

8 Ibid., p. 105.

9 Ibid., p. 97.

10 Ibid., p. 119.

11 Ibid.

12 "The Girl With No Interest in Marriage," *The Colloquies of Erasmus*, p. 106.

13 Ibid., p. 108.

14 See Eric Josef Carlson, *Marriage and the English Reformation*, (NY: Blackwell, 1994), pp. 3-4.

15 Ibid., quoted by Carlson, p. 4.

16 Ibid.

17 Ibid., pp. 4-8.

18 One of the best books on the family in this period is by Steven Ozment entitled *When Fathers Ruled: Family Life in Reformation Europe*, (Cambridge: Harvard University Press, 1983).

19 Lawrence Stone, *The Family, Sex, and Marriage in England: 1500-1800*, (NY: Harper & Row, 1977), p. 7..

20 Ibid., Although Stone may have underestimated here the affective dimensions of the Medieval family, for a different perspective see chapter 3.

21 Ibid., p. 123.

22 Ibid.

23 Ibid., p. 155.

24 Ibid., quoted therein, p. 136.

25 Ibid.

26 Edmund Leites, *The Puritan Conscience and Modern Sexuality*, (New Haven: Yale, 1986), p. 76; cf. also p. 3.

27 Ibid., p. 76.

28 Matthew Griffith, *Bethel: A Forme For Families*, (London: Printed by Richard Badger, 1634), p. 9.

29 Levin L. Schucking, *The Puritan Family: A Social Study From the Literary Sources*, (NY: Schocken Books, 1969), p. 306.

30 Griffith, *Bethel,* p. 9.

31 Ibid., p. 14.

32 Ibid., p. 25.

33 Ibid., pp. 26-27.

34 Ibid., p. 20.

35 Quoted by Edmund S. Morgan, *The Puritan Family: Religion and Domestic Relations in Seventeenth Century New England*, (NY: Harper & Row, 1966), p. 30 from Benjamin Wadsworth, *The Well-Ordered Family*, (Boston, 1712), p. 40.

36 Morgan, *The Puritan Family*, pp. 6-7.

37 Ibid., p. 9.

38 Leites, *The Puritan Conscience*, p. 99.

39 Ibid., p. 34.

40 Ibid., p. 36.

41 John Demos, *A Little Commonwealth: Family Life in Plymouth Colony*, (NY: Oxford University Press, 1970), p. 85.

42 Griffith, *Bethel*, p. 333.

43 Morgan, *The Puritan Family*, p. 45. (In seventeenth century England, women had virtually no right to make contracts, but in Plymouth Colony the courts regularly sustained certain kinds of contracts involving women. See Demos, *A Little Commonwealth*, pp. 85-86).

44 Griffith, *Bethel*, p. 269.

45 Morgan, *The Puritan Family*, p. 31.

46 This system was, of course, ended with the imposition of royal government throughout New England in 1686, after which ministers were empowered to perform the marriage ceremony.

47 Richard Baxter, *A Christian Directory*, 2nd ed., (London, 1678), p. 39.

48 Morgan, *The Puritan Family*, p. 82. It should be noted that in second or later marriages, which were quite common, the financial bargaining was directly done by the engaged partners.

49 Griffith, *Bethel*, p. 28.

50 In F. O. Matthiessen, *The Oxford Book of American Verse*, (NY: Oxford Press, 1950), p. 9.

51 See John Demos, *Past, Present, and Personal: The Family and the Life Course in American History*, (NY: Oxford University Press, 1986), pp. 29-127.

52 Brigitte and Peter Berger, *The War Over the Family: Capturing the Middle Ground*, (NY: Anchor Press, 1983), pp. 87-91.

53 See Martin E. Marty, *Pilgrims in Their Own Land: 500 Years of Religion in America*, (Boston: Little, Brown & Co., 1984), pp. 116-117.

54 Ibid., quoted herein, p. 113.

55 Ibid., p. 119.

56 The observation is that of Nancy F. Cott, *The Bonds of Womanhood: 'Woman's*

Sphere' in New England, 1780-1835, (New Haven: Yale University Press, 1977), p. 129.

57 Ibid., p. 65.

58 Ibid., p. 154.

59 Ibid., quoted by Cott, p. 130.

60 Sennett, *Families Against the City.*

61 Ibid., p. 18.

62 Ibid., p. 20.

63 Ibid., p. 47.

64 Ibid., pp. 50-51.

65 Stone, *Family, Sex, and Marriage*, p. 246. Stone has shown a similar relationship between the authority of husbands and fathers and their participation and leadership in religious activities.

CHAPTER 3:

1 Robert Hanley, "New Jersey Charges Woman, 18, With Killing Baby Born at Prom," *NY Times*, June 24, 1997, pp. A1, B4; Barbara Kantrowitz, "Cradles to Coffins," *Newsweek*, July 7, 1997, pp. 52-54.

2 Michele Ingrassia and John McCormick, "Why Leave Children With Bad Parents," *Newsweek*, April 25, 1994, pp. 52-58.

3 See Chapter One.

4 John Sommerville, *The Rise and Fall of Childhood*, (New York: Vintage Books, 1982), p. 61.

5 John Boswell, *The Kindness of Strangers: The Abandonment of Children in Western Europe From Late Antiquity to the Renaissance*, (New York: Pantheon, 1988), p. 135.

6 See Shulamith Shahar, *Childhood in the Middle Ages*, (London: Routledge, 1990), p. 126.

7 Boswell, *The Kindness of Strangers*, p. 61.

8 Ibid., p. 59.

9 Quoted by Richard B. Lyman from *Barbarism and Religion: Late Roman and Early Medieval Childhood* in Lloyd de Mause ed. *The History of Childhood: The Untold Story of Child Abuse*, (New York: Peter Bedrick Books, 1988), p. 84.

10 Hugh Cunningham, *Children and Childhood in Western Society Since 1500*, (London: Longman, 1995), p. 25.

11 Ibid.

12Ibid.

13 Ibid.

14 Ibid., p. 28.

15 Boswell, *The Kindness of Strangers*, p. 161.

16 Ibid., p. 157. Boswell claims that only a "few Christian moralists" condemned the practice but then demonstrated that nearly all significant Christian authors of the period expressed disapproval of abandonment. Perhaps he means there were only a few Christian writers and they all disapproved but Boswell also has a propensity to minimize the positive impact of Christianity.

17 Ibid., pp. 82-84.

18 Ibid., p. 88.

19 Ibid., p. 158.

20 Ibid., p. 132.

21 I would count John Boswell's excellent work, *The Kindness of Strangers*, as a prime case in point.

22 Boswell, *The Kindness of Strangers*, p. 112.

23 Ibid., p. 113.

24 Beverly Rawson, "Children in the Roman Familia," p. 177 in *The Family in Ancient Rome*, (New York: Cornell University, 1986), pp. 170-200. The author has in mind Trajan (98-117) and Antoninus Pius (137-61).

25 Homilia VII in *Hexaemeron 6* in Boswell, *The Kindness of Strangers*, p.165.

26 Basil, *Homilia in Illud Lucae, Destruam 4*, quoted in Boswell, *The Kindness of Strangers*, pp. 165-66.

27 Cited by Boswell, *The Kindness of Strangers*, p. 167.

28 Ibid., p. 171.

29 Ibid., pp. 167-68.

30 Ibid., pp. 168-69.

31 Ibid., p. 171.

32 Ibid., p. 170.

33 Ibid., p. 172.

34 Lloyd de Mause ed.: *The History of Childhood: The Untold Story of Child Abuse*, (New York: Peter Bedrick Books, 1988), p. 4.

35 Ibid., p. 17.

36 Cunningham, *Children and Childhood*, p. 24.

37 Boswell, *The Kindness of Strangers*, p. 158.

38 Augustine, *The Confessions*, trans. Rex Warner, (New York: NAL, 1963), pp. 23-25.

39 Cunningham, *Children and Childhood*, p. 29.

40 Augustine's belief that the unbaptized infant would be consigned to the fires of hell was not accepted later, and by the twelfth century the notion of limbo for such children, where the child escaped the tortures of hell but also remained bereft of heavenly bliss, was widely held.

41 Shahar, *Childhood in the Middle Ages*, p. 16.

42 Ibid., p. 17.

43 Boswell, *The Kindness of Strangers*, p. 177.

44 Shahar, *Childhood in the Middle Ages*, pp. 172-73.

45 Ibid., p. 173.

46 Mothers were understood to be responsible for the care of children until the age of seven, and then fathers assumed the primary responsibility for boys while mothers continued the education of daughters.

47 Shahar, *Childhood in the Middle Ages*, p. 13

48 Ibid., p. 12.

49 Ibid., p. 117.

50 ell, Ibid., p. 265, n. 26.

51 Boswell, *The Kindness of Strangers*, p. 228.

52 Ibid.

53 Ibid., pp. 232; 244, n. 52. The church, of course, recognized that infants and young children upon reaching maturity would need to make their own commitment to a religious vocation, including the requirement of life-long celibacy. In a society largely devoid of personal choice, however, it is hard to imagine many young adults raised in a monastery exercising this option; from all we know, the alternatives could not have been overwhelmingly appealing.

54 Ibid., pp. 421-3.

55 Recent studies indicate that a considerable percentage of contemporary American infant deaths attributed to SIDS may indeed be the result of child abuse.

56 Mary Martin McLaughlin, "Survivors and Surrogates: Children and Parents From the Ninth to the Thirteenth Centuries," in Lloyd de Mause ed., *The History of Childhood: The Untold Story of Child Abuse*, (New York: Peter Bedrick Books, 1988), p. 120.

57 Ibid.

58 Ibid., p. 121.

59 cf. John Sommerville, *The Rise and Fall of Childhood*, (New York: Vintage Books, 1982), p. 105.

60 Ibid., quoted by Sommerville.

61 Ibid., p. 106.

62 Cunningham, *Children and Childhood*, p. 47.

63 Ibid., p. 49. Cunningham says that over 350 different catechisms were printed in England alone between 1549 and 1646.

64 William Gouge, *Of Domestic Duties*, 1662.

65 See Linda A. Pollock, *Forgotten Children: Parent-Child Relations From 1500-1900*, (Cambridge: Cambridge Univ. Press, 1983), pp. 116; 150-6. Pollock includes Philip Greven's *The Protestant Temperament: Patterns of Child-Rearing, Religious Experience, and the Self in Early America*, (New York: Knopf, 1977) as contributing to the distortion.

66 Pollock, *Forgotten Children*, p. 137.

67 Quoted by Cunningham, *Children and Childhood*, pp. 52-3.

68 Sommerville, *Rise and Fall*, p. 143.

69 Cunningham, *Children and Childhood*, p. 65.

70 Pollock, *Forgotten Children*, pp. 119-20; also 121, 122-3.

71 Ibid., p. 120.

72 Ibid., pp. 120, 122-3.

73 Ibid., p. 172. Pollock notes in the one autobiography, where a child describes actual cruelty of her parents, that they seemed to have been influenced by Locke.

74 Cunningham, *Children and Childhood*, pp. 132-3.

75 Ibid., p. 138. Quoted by Cunningham.

76 Ibid., p. 129.

77 See Walter I. Trattner, *Crusade for the Children: A History of the National Child Labor Committee and Child Labor Reform in America*, (Chicago: Quadrangle Books, 1970).

78 I am grateful to Professor Wilson Kimnach for pointing me to this passage as well as the account of Phebe Bartlet. See Jonathan Edwards, "Some Thoughts Concerning the Revival," in *The Works of Jonathan Edwards*, vol. 4, ed. C. C. Goen, (New Haven: Yale University, 1972), pp. 331-341.

79 Ibid., p. 335.

80 Jonathan Edwards, "A Faithful Narrative," in C. C. Goen, ed., *Works*, pp. 199-205.

81 Ibid., pp. 204-5.

82 See Nancy F. Cott, *The Bonds of Womanhood: Woman's Sphere in New England 1780-1835*, (New Haven: Yale University Press, 1977), p. 86. Cott is very much aware of how the enhanced authority of women in the household served to

add barriers to entry to other public spheres but rightly, in my view, acknowledges that the new domestic role provided the necessary basis for women to challenge its restrictiveness. See pp. 205-6.

83 Ibid., pp. 93-4.

84 Cited by Cunningham from Rousseau's *Emile*, in, *Children and Childhood*, p. 66.

85 Ibid., p. 77.

86 Peter Gregg Slater, *Children in the New England: In Death and In Life*, (Hamden: Archon Books, 1977), pp. 40; 23.

87 Quoted in Slater, *Children in the New England* , p. 154.

88 Ibid., p. 155.

89 Cunningham, *Children and Childhood*, p. 92.

90 Ibid., p. 136.

91 Maureen Fitzgerald, "Charity, Poverty and Welfare" in the *Harvard Divinity Bulletin* 25:4, 1996, pp. 12-17.

92 Ibid., p. 14.

93 Ibid., p. 15.

94 Ibid., p. 16. Fitzgerald states that the average time children spent in Catholic institutions "never exceeded four years.."

95 Ibid.

96 Ibid., p. 12.

97 Trattner, *Crusade for the Children* , p. 27.

98 Ibid., pp. 32-33.

99 Vivianna A. Zelizer, *Pricing the Priceless Child: The Changing Social Value of Children*, (New York: Basic Books, 1985), pp. 58-59.

100 Ibid., p. 5.

101 Ibid., p. 6.

102 Ibid., p. 11.

103 Ibid., p. 142.

104 Ibid., p. 153.

105 Ibid., p. 158. Quoted by Zelizer.

106 Cunningham, *Children and Childhood*, p. 159.

107 Norimitsu Onishi, "Major Moves to Staunch Gang Violence," *New York Times*, Oct. 1997, pp. B1, B3.

108 The evidence is substantial that working children gave either all or almost all of their earned money to their parents in earlier periods.

109 Sommerville, *Rise and Fall*, p. 259.

110 Zelizer, *Priceless Child*, p. 217.

111 Ibid.

CHAPTER 4:

1 By 1985, the Southern Baptists were the only major denomination in which a majority disapproved of premarital sex. See George Gallup, Jr. and Jim Castelli, *The American Catholic People: Their Beliefs, Practices and Values*, Garden City: Doubleday, 1987, p. 51.

2 Andrew Greeley described Catholics in 1985 as the "most affluent Gentile religious group in America." Andrew M. Greeley, *American Catholics Since the Council: An Unauthorized Report*, Chicago: The Thomas Moore Press, 1985, pp. 29-30.

3 46 percent; Gallup and Castelli, *The American Catholic People*, p. 51.

4 The Pope waited two years before issuing his declaration but the surprise rather than lessening may have been increased by the long wait. See Charles R. Morris, *American Catholic: The Saints and Sinners Who Built America's Most Powerful Church*, NY: Times Books, 1997, pp. 361-362.

5 See Andrew M. Greeley, *American Catholics Since the Council: An Unauthorized Report*, Chicago: The Thomas Moore Press, 1985, pp. 55-56, 83-86, 216-217; Jim Bowman, *Bending the Rules: What American Priests Tell American Catholics*, NY: Crossroad, 1994; George Gallup, Jr. and Jim Castelli, *The American Catholic People: Their Beliefs, Practices and Values*, Garden City: Doubleday, 1987; and Charles R. Morris, *American Catholic: The Saints and Sinners Who Built America's Most Powerful Church*, NY: Times Books, 1997, pp. 361-368.

6 Christine Finer Hinze, "Catholic: Family Unity and Diversity Within the Body of Christ," in Phyllis D. Airhart, Margaret Lamberts Bendroth, eds. *Faith Traditions & the Family*, Louisville: Westminster John Knox Press, 1996, pp. 60-63.

7 Ibid., p. 60.

8 *Lumen Gentium*, 1964.

9 *Gaudium Et Spes*, 1965.

10 Karol Wojtyla (Pope John Paul II) undoubtedly was influential in the use of personalist language of *Gaudium Et Spes*.

11 *Fruitful and Responsible Love*, 1979.

12 Homily; Kinshasa, Zaire; 1980.

13 *Familiaris Consortio*, 1981.

14 Ibid.

15 Ibid.

16 It is interestingly right before this point in the document that John Paul II briefly reaffirms "the superiority of this charisma [i.e. celibacy] to marriage." The Pope's understanding is that the successful example of the more highly tested celibate "should strengthen the fidelity of married couples." Ibid.

17 *Familiaris Consortio*, 1981.

18 *Letter to Families*, 1994.

19 *Familiaris Consortio*, 1981.

20 *Letter to Families*, 1994.

21 Ibid.

22 Document on Pastoral Offices, 1965.

23 National Conference of Catholic Bishops (NCCB); August, 2000; on-line <http://nccbuscc.org/LAITY/MARRIAGE/doing:htm#promotion>.

24 on-line <http://NACFLM.org.>.

25 This committee changed its name one more time in 1991 to its present designation as the Secretariat for Family, Laity, Woman and Youth." on-line <http://nccbuscc.org/LAITY/WHOAREWE.htm>.

26 This text was first published in 1988 and updated in 1998. on-line <http://nccbuscc.org/LAITY/MARRIAGE/doing:htm#promotion>.

27 Published by Washington D.C. United States Catholic Conferences, Inc. The Conference also sponsored the 1995 study "Getting It Right: Marriage Preparation in the Catholic Church" conducted by the Center for Marriage and Family, Creighton University, November 1995.

28 See Andrew M. Greeley, *American Catholics Since the Council*, pp. 83-84.

29 Jim Bowman, *Bending the Rules,*

30 Ibid., p. 103.

31 Charles R. Morris, *American Catholic*, p. 365.

32 "Marriage Preparation and Cohabiting Couples: An Information Report on New Realities and Pastoral Practice," 1999, Washington DC United States Catholic Conference, Inc.

33 Ibid.

34 Although McManus has also criticized the Catholic Church for its "failure to address dating couples many of whom opt to live together for a 'trial marriage' before they have become engaged." See Heidi Schlumpf Keymah, "What has the Church Done for Your Marriage Lately?"; *U.S. Catholic*, October, 1993; v. 58, no. 10; p. 30, 31.

35 Ibid., p. 30.

36 A June 29, 1941 instruction from the Holy See, ActApS 33:297, provided specific rules for the required "prenuptial investigation." A handy discussion of Catholic Canon law on marriage can be found in the *New Catholic Encyclopedia* vol. IV, NY: McGraw-Hill, 1967, pp. 271-290.

37 See "Getting it Right: Marriage Preparation in the Catholic Church" (A Study of the Value of Marriage Preparation in the Catholic Church for Couples Married One Through Eight Years), Ibid.

38 See Elizabeth Gleick; "Should This Marriage Be Saved?"; *Time Magazine*, Feb. 27, 1995; pp. 48-56.

39 Ibid., p. 47.

40 "Getting It Right"

41 Ibid.

42 Hinze, "Catholic: Family Unity and Diversity," p. 59.

43 Christine Hinze suggests this bifurcation as a reason for its decline. Although the Vatican, and certainly the American Catholic bishops, have at times emphasized precisely such a dual focus for Catholic families most emphatically in the 1980s. See Lisa Sowle Cahill; "Families Offer Way to Transform Society; love for political justice often begins at home"; *National Catholic Reporter*, March 8, 1996; v. 32; 19; p. 10.

44 See Sue Fox McGovern, "I Do Again," *U.S. Catholic*, May 2000, v. 65, p. 49. It should be mentioned that the CFM maintains a Web site through which it makes several publications available including proceedings of its annual conference.

45 A. H. Clemens, *The Cana Movement in the U.S.*, Wash. DC: Catholic Univ. of America, 1953; also William Richard Clark, ed.; *One in Mind, One in Heart, One in Affections*; Providence: Providence College; 1950.

46 on-line <http://WWME.org/new.html.>.

47 Michael J. McManus, "The Marriage-Saving Movement," *American Entrepreneur*, May/June 1996, v. 7, no. 3, p. 28.

48 on-line <http://WWME.org/>.

49 Ibid.

50 Keymah, "What has the Church Done for Your Marriage Lately?," p. 30.

51 Ibid., p. 32.

52 McManus, "The Marriage-Saving Movement," p. 28.

53 Ibid. And also Elizabeth Gleick; "Should This Marriage Be Saved?"; p. 51.

54 George Gallup, Jr. and Jim Castelli, *The American Catholic People: Their Beliefs, Practices and Values*, Garden City: Doubleday, 1987, p. 42.

55 Alex Garcia-Rivera, "Homemade Faith: The Domestic Church Under

Siege," *U.S. Catholic*, Nov. 1994, v. 59, no. 11, p. 50.

56 Patricia Lefevere; "Familyland: A Cultural Detox and Spiritual Warfare Training Center"; *National Catholic Reporter*, Oct. 3, 1997; v. 33, no. 42, p. 3.

57 Soon after launching his Apostolate, Coniker met the late Mother Teresa, who was the top champion of the Coniker's ministry. See "Regular Travel Between Rome and Remote Center"; *National Catholic Reporter*, Oct. 3, 1997; v. 33, no. 42, p. 5.

58 Patricia Lefevere, "Familyland," p. 4.

59 Ibid.

60 Ibid.

61 "Regular Travel."

62 Joseph W. Hinkle, "Strengthening Families: A Challenge of the 1980's" in *Baptist History and Heritage* v.117, Jan. 1982, p. 1.

63 J. Clark Hensley, "Trends in Baptist Family Life" in *Baptist History and Heritage*, v.117, Jan. 1982, p. 10.

64 G. Wade Rowatt, Jr. and Dianne Bertolino-Green, "Family Ministries Among Southern Baptists" in *Baptist History and Heritage* v.117, Jan. 1982, p. 16.

65 Reuben Herring, "Southern Baptist Convention Resolutions on the Family" in *Baptist History and Heritage* v.117, Jan. 1982, p. 36.

66 See Rowatt and Bertolino-Green, "Family Ministries," p.14.

67 Ibid.

68 Ibid.

69 *Annual*, Southern Baptist Convention (SBC), 1941, p. 306.

70 Ibid., 1945, p. 331.

71 Rowatt and Bertolino-Green, "Family Ministries," p. 15.

72 Bill J. Leonard, "Southern Baptists: Family as Witness of Grace in the Community" in Phyllis D. Airhart and Margaret Lamberts Bendroth eds., *Faith Traditions and the Family*, Louisville: Westminster John Knox Press, 1996.

73 *Annual*, SBC, 1968, p. 238.

74 Leonard, "Southern Baptists: Family as Witness," p. 13.

75 Rowatt and Bertolino-Green, "Family Ministries," p. 16.

76 Ibid., p. 21.

77 Ibid., p. 16.

78 Ibid., p. 17.

79 Hinkle, "Strengthening Families," p. 2.

80 *Annual*, SBC, 1975, p. 74.

81 Hinkle, "Strengthening Families," p. 2.

82 Ibid.

83 Ibid., p. 6.

84 Bill J. Leonard, *God's Last and Only Hope: The Fragmentation of the Southern Baptist Convention*, Grand Rapids: Wm. B. Eerdmans, 1990, p. 4.

85 Leonard speaks of the uniformity in perspective between the broader conservative Southern culture and the SBC historically and at present. Ibid.; pp. xi, 13-17.

86 *Annual*, SBC, 1977, p. 52.

87 "Southern Baptists Vote to Boycott Disney"; *The Christian Century* v. 114; July 2-9, 1997; pp. 623-24.

88 Ibid., p. 623.

89 A third organization called the Brotherhood was also folded into the NAMB at the same time.

90 "SBC Approves Family Statement"; *The Christian Century* v. 115; June 17-24, 1998; p. 602.

91 Ibid.

92 All information is from the official SBC NAMB website.

93 Ibid.

94 Ibid.

95 Ibid.

96 Ibid.

97 "HelpLink"; North American Mission Board (NAMB); May, 2000; on-line <http://namb.net/helplink>.

98 Ibid.

99 Ibid.

100 Ibid.

101 Ibid., on-line <http://namb.net/helplink/familyidx.asp>.

102 Ibid. , on-line <http://namb.net/helplink/SX_MARR.asp>.

103 Ibid.

104 Ibid. , on-line <http://namb.net/helplink/SXIMPNT.asp>.

105 Ibid.

106 Ibid. , on-line <http://namb.net/helplink/SX_CPS.asp>.

107 Ibid.

108 Ibid. , on-line <http://namb.net/helplink/SX_DATE.asp>.

109 Ibid.

110 Ibid.

111 John Zipperer, "'True Love Waits' Now Worldwide Effort"; *Christianity Today* v.38; July 18, 1994; p. 58.

112 Ibid.

113 Gracie S. Hsu, "The Revolt of the Virgins," *The World and I*, Dec. 1996, p. 53.

114 See George Gallup, Jr. and Jim Castelli, *The American Catholic People: Their Beliefs, Practices and Values*, Garden City: Doubleday, 1987. More Southern Baptists indicate awareness of, or influence by "a presence or a power-whether you call it God" (p.14); are involved in evangelization (p.17), and tithe to their church (p.39) than members of either other mainline Protestant denominations or the Roman Catholic Church.

CHAPTER 5:

1 In B. Carmon Hardy, *Solemn Covenant: The Mormon Polygamous Passage*, Chicago: Univ. of Illinois Press, 1992, quoted on p. 294.

2 Ibid.

3 Ibid., p. 268.

4 Jan Shipps, *Mormonism: The Story of a New Religious Tradition*, Urbana: Univ. of Illinois, 1985, p. 38.

5 Ibid., p. 61.

6 Klaus J. Hansen, "Mormonism and the American Experience" in the *Chicago History of American Religion*, Martin E. Marty ed., Chicago: Univ. of Chicago, 1981, p. 164.

7 Shipps, *New Religious Tradition*, p. 134.

8 Hardy, *Covenant*, p. 14.

9 Hardy describes their efforts as apologetic, my own study of the early Christian apologetic tradition suggests that such apologetics are motivated centrally by evangelical commitment. See A. J. Guerra, *Romans and the Apologetic Tradition*, Cambridge: Cambridge University, 1995.

10 Hardy, *Covenant*, p. 87.

11 Ibid., p. 15.

12 Hansen, *Mormonism*, p. 165.

13 Ibid., p. 167.

14 Ibid., p. 168.

15 Ibid., p. 89.

16 Or perhaps more problematic. Ibid.

17 Hardy, *Covenant*, p. 17.

18 Ibid.

19 Ibid., pp. 46-47.

20 Ibid., p. 130.

21 Ibid., p. 247.

22 Ibid., pp. 174-176.

23 Hansen, *Mormonism*, p. 176.

24 See Hansen, *Mormonism*, pp. 155-156; Hardy, *Covenant*, pp. 5; 11-12.

25 Hardy, *Covenant*, p. 7.

26 Ibid., p. 298.

27 Ibid., p. 338.

28 All references are to Larry L. Jensen and Ronald S. Jackson, "A Theory of Caring: Predicting Gender and Role Differences in a Religious Setting," p. 5. I am grateful to Dr. Jensen for sharing this paper with me before its publication.

29 Ibid.

30 Quotation from Jensen and Jackson, "A Theory of Caring," p. 5-6.

31 Quotation from Jensen and Jackson, "A Theory of Caring," p. 6.

32 Ibid.

33 Ibid.

34 Mary Farrell Bednarowski, *New Religions and the Theological Imagination in America*, Bloomington: Indiana Univ. Press, 1989, p. 99.

35 The best available biography of the Rev. Moon in English is by the British author Michael Breen, *Sun Myung Moon: The Early Years 1920-53*, West Sussex: Refuge Books, 1997. A competent treatment of the Asian context for the Unification Church is to be found in George D. Chryssides, *The Advent of Sun Myung Moon: The Origins, Beliefs and Practices of the Unification Church*, London: Macmillan, 1991, especially pp. 7-88.

36 Eileen Barker, *The Making of a Moonie: Choice or Brainwashing?*, Oxford: Basil Blackwell, 1984, p. 3.

37 James A. Beckford, *Cult Controversy: The Societal Response to New Religious Movements*, London: Tavistock, 1985, pp. 42-43.

38 Joseph H. Fichter, *The Holy Family of Father Moon*, Kansas City: Leaven Press, 1985, pp. 61-62.

39 Ibid., p. 62.

40 Ibid., cited by Fichter.

41 Sun Myung Moon, *Blessing and Ideal Family*, NY: HSA-UWC Publications, 1993, p. 21.

42 His numerous sermons are strewn with encouragement for those in blessed marriages to kiss long, have long intercourse, etc.

43 W. Farley Jones, *True Love and World Peace*, Troy, NY, Feb. 1993.

44 Ibid.

45 Ibid.

46 Ibid., quoted by Jones.

47 See Farley and Betsy Jones eds., *Raising Children of Peace*, NY: HSA-UWC Publications, 1997.

48 Peter F. Brown, "The Eternal Castle of True Love" in F. and B. Jones eds., *Raising Children of Peace*, P. 37.

49 Ibid., pp. 37-38.

50 Ibid., p. 38. Of course, many Unification couples do not begin in love but, as in many arranged marriages that succeed, develop spousal love over an extended period of time.

51 In Unification understanding this is Sun Myung Moon and his wife, Hak Ja Han, in the position of the restored Adam and Eve.

52 See George D. Chryssides, *The Advent of Sun Myung Moon: The Origins, Beliefs and Practices of the Unification Church*, London: Macmillan, 1991, p. 131.

53 The media, of course, coined the term "mass marriage" whereas the movement's self-understanding would more appropriately be reflected in the term "joint marriages."

54 Sun Myung Moon, *Blessing and Ideal Family*, p. 223.

55 A separate much smaller mass wedding of 43 couples including Japanese as well as Westerners was held shortly after the 430 couples mass wedding. It should be noted that except for Korea the movement was very young and tiny in all countries in the 1960s when these first several mass marriages were taking place.

56 One of the most significant factors in the widespread persecution of the Unification Church has been the disgruntlement of parents whose children married partners of an unacceptable race or nationality.

57 Eileen Barker, *The Making of a Moonie: Choice or Brainwashing?*, Oxford: Basil Blackwell, 1984, p. 193.

58 Ibid., p. 215. Barker observes that about a quarter of the Moonies compared to about five percent of the general British population went to fee-paying schools.

59 George D. Chryssides, *The Advent of Sun Myung Moon*, pp. 6-7.

60 Eileen Barker, *The Making of a Moonie*, p. 244.

61 Ibid., pp. 220; 227.

62 Ibid., p. 210.

63 Joseph Fichter, *The Holy Family of Father Moon*, pp. 111-123.

64 James A. Beckford, *Cult Controversy*, p. 80.

65 See "Gated Religions," *Christian Century*, 114:13, April 16, 1997, p. 382, where in addition to its control of the *Washington Times*, Unification-sponsored family values conferences are cited as evidence of its becoming "integrated into the mainstream of religious life." The article notes that these conferences held around the globe attract "world leaders and such well-known figures as Ralph Reed of the Christian Coalition."

66 There are, of course, some unflattering characterizations of Sun Myung Moon. A long-standing accusation is that he formerly engaged in sexual purification rites with female members of his church. Indeed, at least a few leaders of messianic Korean religious movements in this century have apparently practiced this rite, known as *P'i Kareun* in Korean (See George D. Chryssides, *The Advent of Sun Myung Moon*, p. 146). However, the several Western scholars who have investigated this charge as levied against Rev. Moon have concluded it to be unfounded (Frederick Sontag, *Sun Myung Moon and the Unification Church*, Nashville: Abingdon, 1977; G. Kehrer ed., *Das Entstehen einer Neuen Religion: das Beispiel der Vereinigungskirche*, München, Köesel-Verlag, 1981).

How do Unificationists respond to the litany of continuing accusations against their spiritual leader—some recently given wider play in the American media (See Nansook Hong, *In the Shadow of the Moons: My Life in the Reverend Sun Myung Moon's Family*, Boston: Little, Brown & Co., 1998)? It is widely known that the Rev. Moon was previously married and divorced. The accepted explanation within the Unification movement is that the Rev. Moon's first wife was unable to embrace her husband's religious mission, leading her to file for divorce. Recently, an allegation has arisen that Sun Myung Moon fathered an illegitimate son sometime in the 1960s in the United States (This allegation was reviewed on a broadcast of the *60 Minutes* program in Sept. 1998 and occurs in Hong's book *In the Shadow of the Moons*). While some Unificationists peremptorily dismiss any such allegations, others seem to have responded much like sophisticated Mormon believers accept their founder's polygamous relationships while they staunchly uphold the sanctity of life-long monogamous marriage. An unofficial biography recounts Rev. Moon heroically risking his life on several occasions in order to fulfill his understanding of the Will of God (See Michael Breen, *Sun Myung Moon: The Early Years 1920-53*, West Sussex: Refuge Books, 1997). It would appear that Rev. Moon's characteristic devotion may be one of the bases for faithful Unificationists to keep any alleged early transgressions by their leader in perspective and even to believe, as some appear to, that the mission requirements of certain providential figures can lead to actions that contradict conventional morality (See Soren Kierkegaard, Alastair Hannay trans., *Fear and Trembling*, England: Penguin Books Ltd., 1987. Kierkegaard developed the concept of the "teleological suspension of the ethical" as an explanation of the religious act exemplified in Abraham's willingness to obey God's commandment to kill his own son, Isaac. This argument has been directly advanced in at least one internet discussion group of Unificationist intellectuals).

67 Moon, Sun Myung, 'The Ideal Spouse', February 4, 1969, Tokyo, Japan, p. 20 in *God's Will and the World*, NY: HSA-UWC, 1985.

68 Moon, Sun Myung, 'In Search of the Origin of the Universe', August 1, 1996, Washington, DC, pp. 21-22 in *True Love and True Family*, NY: FFWPU, 1997.

69 Moon, Sun Myung, 'The Ideal Spouse', p. 21.

70 The sermons of Rev. Moon occupy nearly two hundred volumes and it is from this massive material that the family reading material has been culled.

71 Family Pledge card, NY: HSA-UWC.

72 Joseph H. Fichter, *The Holy Family of Father Moon*, p. 99.

73 Unificationists, however, do not believe their children's spiritual perfection is guaranteed for their teachings pronounces every individual should fulfill his/her own "portion of responsibility." See *Exposition of the Divine Principle*, NY: HSA-UWC, 1996, chapter one.

74 Peter F. Brown, "Resurrecting and Uplifting Our Children's Hearts," in Farley and Betsy Jones eds., *Raising Children of Peace*, NY: HSA-UWC Publications, 1997, p. 189.

75 Bill McCartney with Dave Diles, *From Ashes to Glory*, Nashville: Thomas Nelson Publishers, 1995, p. 286.

76 Ken Abraham, *Who Are the Promise Keepers? : Understanding the Christian Men's Movement*, NY: Doubleday, 1997, p. 17.

77 Ibid., p. 18.

78 McCartney, *From Ashes to Glory*, p. 288.

79 Ibid., p. 289.

80 John D. Spaulding, 'Bonding in the Bleachers: A Visit to the Promise Keepers', *Christian Century* 113:8, March 6, 1996, p. 263.

81 Art Moore, 'More Promise Keepers Downsizing', *Christianity Today*, 42:1, October 5, 1998, pp. 20-21.

82 Abraham, *Who Are the Promise Keepers?*, p. 13.

83 Ibid., p. 12.

84 See Kenneth L. Woodward, 'The Gospel of Guyhood', *Newsweek*, August 29, 1994, pp. 60-61.

85 Abraham, *Who Are the Promise Keepers?*, p. 21.

86 Ibid., p. 33.

87 Bill McCartney with David Halbrook, *Sold Out: Becoming Man Enough to Make a Difference*, Nashville: Ward Publishing, 1997, p. 315.

88 Quotation from Ken Abraham, *Who Are the Promise Keepers?*, P. 43.

89 Ibid., p. 49.

90 McCartney, *Sold Out*, p. 170.

91 See Marci McDonald, 'My wife told me to go: Why Promise Keepers is thriving despite feminists' warnings', *U.S. News & World Report*, October 6, 1997, pp. 28, 30.

92 Ibid.

93 Ibid., p. 28.

94 Ibid., quotation from p. 30.

95 Douglas DeCelle, 'Among the Promise Keepers: A Pastor's Reflections', *Christian Century* 113: 21, July 3-10, 1996, p. 696.

96 Abraham, *Who Are the Promise Keepers?*, p. 145.

97 McCartney fasted for forty days for this event. McCartney, *Sold Out*, p. 275.

98 DeCelle, 'Among the Promise Keepers', p. 695.

99 Ibid., p. 696.

100 McCartney, *Sold Out*, p. 315.

101 Ibid., p. 179.

102 Abraham, *Who Are the Promise Keepers?*, p. 124.

103 McCartney, *Sold Out*, p. 177.

104 Ibid.

105 Ibid., p. 178.

106 Ibid., p. 180.

107 Spaulding, 'Bonding in the Bleachers', p. 264.

108 Abraham, *Who Are the Promise Keepers?*, p. 128.

109 McCartney, *Sold Out*, p. 178. "…God's heart is for the full complement of His people to be gathered in His name, represented in all the incalculably rich, heavenly splendor of racial and cultural diversity."

110 Ibid., p. 181.

111 See 'Hundreds of thousands of Christian men gather on Mall in Washington', *New York Times*, October 5, 1997, 11. The *Times* compared the event to the civil rights rally three decades before.

112 Moore, 'More Promise Keepers Downsizing', p. 20-21.

113 Ibid.

114 Ibid., p. 21.

115 Abraham, *Who Are the Promise Keepers?*, p. 35.

116 McCartney, *Sold Out*, p. 270.

117 McCartney, *From Ashes to Glory*, p. 93.

118 McCartney, *Sold Out*, p. 185.

CONCLUSION:

1 Warren Hoge, "Royals' Golden Day, Graced by Common Touch," *N.Y. Times*, Nov. 21, 1997, p. A 4.

2 See Thomas Reeves, *The Empty Church: The Suicide of Liberal Christianity*, NY: The Free Press, 1996 and Donald E. Miller, *Reinventing American Protestantism: Christianity in the New Millennium*, Berkeley: Univ. of California, 1997.

3 Coventry Patmore, *The Angel in the House*, London: George Bell & Sons, 1878. This nineteenth-century British work was required reading for school children well into the twentieth century. The "angel" in the house refers to the wife and mother who is now seen as the paragon of virtue and piety.

Bibliography

Abraham, Ken. *Who Are the Promise Keepers?: Understanding the Christian Men's Movement.* NY: Doubleday, 1997.

Airhart, Phyllis D. and Margaret Lamberts Bendroth. *Faith, Traditions and the Family.* Kentucky: Westminster John Knox Press, 1996.

Alvarez, Helen. "Behind the Drop in Teen-age Births." *The New York Times,* 4 May 1999, p. A30.

Apple, R. W. "His Battle Now Lost, Moynihan Still Cries Out." *The New York Times.* 2 Aug. 1996, p. A16.

Aquinas, Thomas. *The Truth of the Catholic Faith.* trans. Vernon J. Bourke. Garden City: Doubleday, 1956.

Augustine. *The Confessions.* trans. Rex Warner. New York: NAL, 1963.

Bahr, Howard M. and Bruce A. Chadwick. "Religion and Family in Middletown, U.S.A." *Journal of Marriage and Family.* 47, No. 2, May 1985: pp. 407-414.

Barker, Eileen. *The Making of a Moonie: Choice or Brainwashing?* Oxford: Basil Blackwell, 1984.

Baxter, Richard. *A Christian Directory.* 2nd ed. London: 1678.

Beckford, James A. *Cult Controversy: The Societal Response to New Religious Movements.* London: Tavistock, 1985.

Bednarowski, Mary Farrell. *New Religions and the Theological Imagination in America.* Bloomington: Indiana University Press, 1989.

Berger, Brigitte and Peter Berger. *The War Over the Family: Capturing the Middle Ground.* NY: Anchor Press, 1983.

Boswell, John. *The Kindness of Strangers: The Abandonment of Children in Western Europe From Late Antiquity to the Renaissance.* New York: Pantheon, 1988.

Bowman, Jim. Bending the Rules: *What American Priests Tell American Catholics.* New York: Crossroad, 1994.

Breen, Michael. *Sun Myung Moon: The Early Years 1920-53.* West Sussex: Refuge Books, 1997.

Brown, Peter. "Late Antiquity." *A History of Private Life.* Vol. 1, eds. Aries and Duby. Cambridge: Belknap Press, 1987, pp. 251-309.

Brown, Peter F. "Resurrecting and Uplifting Our Children's Hearts." *Raising Children of Peace.* eds. W. Farley and Betsy Jones. NY: HSA-UWC Publications, 1997, pp. 187-190.

———. "The Eternal Castle of True Love." *Raising Children of Peace.* eds. W. Farley and Betsy Jones. NY: HSA-UWC Publications, 1997, pp. 35-39.

Browning, Don S., et al. *From Culture Wars to Common Ground.* Kentucky: Westminster John Knox Press, 1997.

Cahill, Lisa Sowle. "Families Offer Way to Transform Society: Love for Political Justice Often Begins at Home." *National Catholic Reporter.* 32, No. 19, 8 March 1996: p. 10.

Caplow, Theodore, et al. *Middletown Families: Fifty Years of Change and Continuity.* Minneapolis: University of Minnesota, 1982.

Carlson, Allan. "The Family: Where Do We Go From Here?" *Transaction: Social Science and Modern Society.* 32, No. 5, July/Aug. 1995: p. 65.

Carlson, Eric Josef. *Marriage and the English Reformation.* New York: Blackwell, 1994.

Carr, Anne and Mary Stewart Van Leeuwen eds. *Religion, Feminism, and the Family.* Kentucky: Westminster John Knox Press, 1996.

Children of Our Time: The Children of the Fourth World. Symposium Series, vol. 7. NY: Edwin Mellen Press, 1981.

Chryssides, George D. T*he Advent of Sun Myung Moon: The Origins, Beliefs and Practices of the Unification Church.* London: Macmillan, 1991.

Clark, Richard, ed. *One in Mind, One in Heart, One in Affections.* Providence: Providence College, 1950.

Clemens, A. H. *The Cana Movement in the U. S.* Washington D.C.: Catholic University of America, 1953.

Cott, Nancy F. *The Bonds of Womanhood: 'Woman's Sphere' in New England, 1780-1835.* New Haven: Yale University Press, 1977.

Critchlow, Donald T. *Intended Consequences: Birth Control, Abortion and the Federal Government in Modern America.* New York: Oxford University, 1999.

Cunningham, Hugh. *Children and Childhood in Western Society Since 1500.* London: Longman, 1995.

DeCelle, Douglas. "Among the Promise Keepers: A Pastor's Reflections." *Christian Century,* 113:21, 3-10 July, 1996, pp. 695-696.

Deming, Will. Paul on Marriage and Celibacy: T*he Hellenistic Background of I Corinthians 7.* Cambridge: Cambridge University Press, 1995.

Demos, John. *A Little Commonwealth: Family Life in Plymouth Colony.* New York: Oxford University Press, 1970.

Demos, John. *Past, Present and Personal: The Family and the Life Course in American History.* New York: Oxford University Press, 1986.

Doyle, Roger. Atlas of Contemporary America: A Portrait of the Nation. New York: Facts on File, June 1994.

Duby, Georges. The Knight, the Lady and the Priest: The Making of Modern Marriage in Medieval France. trans. Barbara Bray. New York: Pantheon Books. 1983.

Edmonds, V. H. "Marital Conventionalization: Definition and Measurement." *Journal of Marriage and Family.* Vol. 29, 1968, pp. 681-688.

Edwards, Jonathan. "A Faithful Narrative." *The Works of Jonathan Edwards.* ed. C. C. Goen. New Haven: Yale University, 1972, pp. 199-205.

Edwards, Jonathan. "Some Thoughts Concerning the Revival." Vol. 4 of *The Works of Jonathan Edwards.* ed. C. C. Goen. New Haven: Yale University, 1972, pp. 331-341.

Erasmus, Desiderius. *The Colloquies of Erasmus.* trans. Craig R. Thompson. Chicago: University of Chicago, 1965.

Fichter, Joseph H. *The Holy Family of Father Moon.* Kansas City: Leaven Press, 1985.

Field, James. "The Purpose of the Lex Julia et Papia-Poppaea." *Classical Journal,* Vol. 4, 1944/45: p. 400.

Filsinger, Erik E. and Margaret R. Wilson. "Religiosity, Socio-economic Reward and Family Development: Predictors of Marital Adjustment." *Journal of Marriage and Family,* 46, No. 3 Aug. 1984: pp. 663-670.

Fitzgerald, Maureen. "Charity, Poverty and Welfare." Harvard Divinity Bulletin, 25, No. 4, 1996, pp. 12-17.

Frank, Richard I. "Augustus' Legislation on Marriage and Children." *California Studies in Classical Antiquity*, Vol. 8, 1975: pp. 41-43.

Gallup, George Jr. and Jim Castelli. *The American Catholic People:Their Beliefs, Practices and Values*. Garden City: Doubleday, 1987.

Garcia-Rivera, Alex. "Homemade Faith: The Domestic Church Under Siege." *U.S. Catholic*, 59, No. 11, 1994, p. 50.

Gardella, Peter. *Innocent Ecstasy: How Christianity Gave America an Ethic of Sexual Pleasure*. New York: Oxford University, 1985.

"Gated Religions." *Christian Century*, 114:13, 16 April, 1997, p. 382.

Gleick, Elizabeth. "Should This Marriage be Saved?" *Time Magazine*, 27 Feb.1995, pp. 47-56.

Gouge, William. *Of Domestic Duties*. 1662.

Greeley, Andrew M.. *American Catholics Since the Council: An Unautho-rized Report*. Chicago: The Thomas Moore Press, 1985.

Greenwood, Peter W. "Juvenile Crime and Juvenile Justice." *Crime*. eds. James Q. Wilson and Joan Petersilia. San Francisco: ICS Press, 1995, pp. 91-117.

Greven, Philip. *The Protestant Temperament: Patterns of Child-Rearing, Religious Experience, and the Self in Early America*. New York: Knopf, 1977.

Griffith, Matthew. Bethel: *A Forme for Families*. London: Richard Badger, 1634.

Guerra, Anthony J. *Romans and the Apologetic Tradition: The Purpose, Genre and Meaning of Paul's Letter*. Cambridge: Cambridge University, 1995.

Guerra, Anthony J. "The Conversion of Marcus Aurelius and Justin Martyr." *The Second Century*, 9, No. 3, 1992.

Hammond, Phillip E., Mark A. Shibley and Peter M. Solow. "Religion and Family Values in Presidential Voting." *Sociology of Religion*, 55, No. 3, 1994: pp. 277-290.

Hanley, Robert. "New Jersey Charges Woman, 18, With Killing Baby Born at Prom." *The New York Times*, 24 June 1997, pp. A1, B4.

Hansen, Gary L. "Marital Adjustment and Conventionalization: A Re-Examination." *Journal of Marriage and Family*, Vol. 43, Nov. 1981: pp. 855-863.

Hansen, Klaus J. "Mormonism and the American Experience." *Chicago History of American Religion.* ed. Martin E. Marty. Chicago: University of Chicago, 1981 pp. 155-176.

Hardy, B. Carmon. *Solemn Covenant: The Mormon Polygamous Passage.* Chicago: University of Illinois Press, 1992.

Hensley, J. Clark. "Trends in Baptist Family Life." *Baptist History and Heritage,* Vol. 117, Jan. 1982, p. 10.

Herring, Reuben. "Southern Baptist Convention Resolutions on the Family." *Baptist History and Heritage,* Vol. 117, Jan. 1982, p. 36.

Hinkle, Joseph W. "Strengthening Families: A Challenge of the 1980s." *Baptist History and Heritage,* Vol. 117, Jan. 1982, pp. 1-6.

Hinze, Christine Finer. "Catholic: Family Unity and Diversity Within the Body of Christ." *Faith Traditions and the Family.* eds. Phyllis D. Airhart and Margaret Lamberts Bendroth. Louisville: Westminster John Knox Press, 1996 pp. 59-63.

Hirschi, Travis. "The Family." *Crime.* ed. James Q. Wilson and Joan Petersilia. San Francisco: ICS Press, 1995 pp. 121-140.

Hoge, Warren. "Royal's Golden Day, Graced by Common Touch." *The New York Times,* 14 Nov. 1997, p. A4.

Holmes, Steven A. "Birth Rate Falls to 40-Year Low Among Unwed Black Women." *The New York Times,* 1 July 1998, p. A1.

Holy Spirit Association for the Unification of World Christianity (HSA-UWC). *Exposition of the Divine Principle.* NY: HSA-UWC, 1996, Ch. 1.

Hong, Nansook. *In the Shadow of the Moons: My Life in the Reverend Sun Myung Moon's Family.* Boston: Little, Brown & Co., 1998.

Hsu, Gracie S. "The Revolt of the Virgins." *The World and I,* Dec. 1996, p.53.

"Hundreds of Thousands of Christian Men Gather on Mall in Washington." *The New York Times,* 5 October, 1997, p. I1.

Hunter, David G. trans. & ed. *Marriage in the Early Church.* Minneapolis: Fortress Press, 1992.

Ingrassia, Michele and John McCormick. "Why Leave Children With Bad Parents." *Newsweek,* 25 April, 1994, pp. 52-58.

Jenkins, Kip W. "Religion and Families." Vol. 1 of *Family Research: A Sixty-Year Review*, 1930-1990. ed. Stephen J. Bahr. New York: Lexington Books, 1991, pp. 235-238.

Jensen, Larry and Janet Jensen. "Family Values, Religiosity and Gender." *Psychology Reports*, Vol. 73, 1993: pp. 429-430.

Jensen, Larry L. and Ronald S. Jackson. "A Theory of Caring: Predicting Gender and Role Differences in a Religious Setting."

Johnson, M. A. "Family Life and Religious Commitment." *Review of Religious Research*, Vol. 14, 1973: pp. 165-180.

Johnson, Paul. "God and the Americas." *Commentary*, 99, No. 1, Jan. 1995, pp. 25-45.

Jones, W. Farley. *True Love and World Peace*. Troy, NY. 1993.

Kantrowitz, Barbara. "Cradles to Coffins." *Newsweek*, 7 July 1997, pp. 52-54.

Kehrer, G. ed. *Das Entstehen einer Nuen Religion: das Beispel der Vereinigungskirche*. München: Köesel-Verlag, 1981.

Keymah, Heidi Schlumpf. "What has the Church Done for Your Marriage Lately?" *U.S. Catholic*, 58, No. 10, Oct. 1993, pp. 30-32.

Kierkegaard, Soren. *Fear and Trembling*. trans. Alastair Hannay. England: Penguin Books, 1997.

Laumann, Edward O., et al. *The Social Organization of Sexuality: Sexual Practices in the United States*. Chicago: The University of Chicago Press, 1994.

Lefevere, Patricia. "Familyland: A Cultural Detox and Spiritual Warfare Training Center." *National Catholic Reporter*, 33, No. 42, 3 Oct. 1997, p. 3.

Leites, Edmund. *The Puritan Conscience and Modern Sexuality*. New Haven: Yale, 1986.

Leonard, Bill J. *God's Last and Only Hope: The Fragmentation of the Southern Baptist Convention*. Grand Rapids: Wm. B. Eerdmans, 1990.

Leonard, Bill J. "Southern Baptists: Family as Witness of Grace in the Community." *Faith Traditions and the Family*. eds. Phyllis D. Airhart and Margaret Lamberts Bendroth. Louisville: Westminster John Knox Press, 1996 p. 13.

Levitan, Sar A. and Richard S. Belous. *What's Happening to the American Family?* Baltimore: The Johns Hopkins University, 1981.

Lyman, Richard B. "Barbarism and Religion: Late Roman and Early Medieval Childhood." *The History of Childhood: The Untold Story of Child Abuse.* ed. Lloyd de Mause. New York: Peter Bedrick Books, 1988.

MacMullen, Ramsey. *Christianizing the Roman Empire.* New Haven: Yale, 1984.

Marty, Martin E. *Pilgrims in Their Own Land:* 500 Years of Religion in America. Boston: Little, Brown & Co. 1984.

Matthiessen, F. O. *The Oxford Book of American Verse.* New York: Oxford Press, 1950.

Mause, Lloyd de. *The History of Childhood: The Untold Story of Child Abuse.* New York: Peter Bedrick Books, 1988, pp. 4, 17.

May, Elaine Tyler. "Myths and Realities of the American Family." *A History of Private Life: Riddles of Identity in Modern Times.* eds. Antoine Prost and Gerard Vincente. Boston: Harvard University Press, 1991.

McCartney, Bill and Dave Diles. *From Ashes to Glory.* Nashville: Thomas Nelson Publishers, 1995.

McCartney, Bill and David Halbrook. *Sold Out: Becoming Man Enough to Make a Difference.* Nashville: Ward Publishing, 1997.

McDonald, Marci. "My Wife Told Me to Go: Why Promise Keepers is Thriving Despite Feminists' Warnings." *U.S. News & World Report,* 6 October, 1997, pp. 28, 30.

McGovern, Sue Fox. "I Do Again." *U.S. Catholic,* Vol. 65, May 2000: p. 49.

McLanahan, Sara S. "The Consequences of Single Motherhood." *The American Prospect,* Summer 1994: pp. 48-58.

McLaughlin, Mary Martin. "Survivors and Surrogates: Children and Parents From the Ninth to the Thirteenth Centuries." *The History of Childhood: The Untold Story of Child Abuse.* ed. Lloyd de Mause. New York: Peter Bedrick Books, 1988, p. 120-121.

McManus, Michael T. "The Marriage Saving Movement." *American Entrepreneur,* 7, No.3, May/June 1996: pp. 28.

Miller, Donald E. *Reinventing American Protestantism: Christianity in the New Millennium.* Berkeley: University of California, 1997.

Moon, Sun Myung. *Blessing and Ideal Family.* NY: HSA-UWC Publications, 1993.

————. *God's Will and the World.* NY: HSA-UWC, 1985.

————. *True Love and True Family.* NY: FFWPU, 1997.

Moore, Art. "More Promise Keepers Downsizing." *Christianity Today,* 42:1, 5, October, 1998: pp. 20-21.

Morgan, Edmund S. *The Puritan Family: Religion and Domestic Relations in Seventeenth Century New England.* New York: Harper & Row, 1966.

Morris, Charles R. *American Catholic: The Saints and Sinners Who Built America's Most Powerful Church.* New York: Times Books, 1997.

Murstein, Bernard I. *Love, Sex and Marriage Through the Ages.* New York: Springer, 1974.

National Association of Catholic Family Life Ministers [online]. Aug. 2000. Available from World Wide Web: <http://NACFLM.org>.

National Conference of Catholic Bishops (NAMB) [online]. Aug. 2000. Available from World Wide Web: *<http://nccbuscc.org>.*

New Catholic Encyclopedia. Vol. IV, New York: McGraw-Hill, 1967.

North American Mission Board (NAMB) [on line]. May 2000. Available from World Wide Web: *<http://namb.net>.*

Onishi, Norimitsu. "Major Moves to Staunch Gang Violence." *The New York Times,* Oct. 1997, pp. B1, B3.

Ozment, Steven. *When Fathers Ruled: Family Life in Reformation Europe.* Cambridge: Harvard University Press, 1983.

Pagels, Elaine. *Adam, Eve and the Serpent.* New York: Random House, 1989.

Parrinder, Geoffrey. *Sex in the World's Religions.* New York: Oxford University, 1980.

Pamore, Coventry. *The Angel in the House.* London: George Bell & Sons, 1878.

Peterson, Peter G. "Will America Grow Up Before It Grows Old?" *The Atlantic Monthly,* 1 May 1996, p. 57.

"Poll Reveals More Acceptance of a Changing American Family." *The New York Times*, 26 November, 1999, p. A41.

Pollock, Linda A. Forgotten Children: *Parent-Child Relations From 1500-1900*. Cambridge: Cambridge University Press, 1983.

Rawson, Beverly. "Children in the Roman Familia." *The Family in Ancient Rome*. New York: Cornell University, 1986, pp. 170-200.

Rector, Robert. "God and the Underclass." *National Review*, 48, No. 13, 15 July 1996: pp. 30-33.

Reeves, Thomas. *The Empty Church: The Suicide of Liberal Christianity*. New York: The Free Press, 1996.

"Regular Travel Between Rome and Remote Center." *National Catholic Reporter*, 33, No.42, 3 Oct. 1997, p. 5.

Reich, Robert B. *The Work of Nations: Preparing Ourselves for Twenty-First Century Capitalism*. New York: Alfred A. Knopf, 1991.

Rowatt, G. Wade Jr. and Dianne Bertolino-Green. "Family Ministries Among Southern Baptists." *Baptist History and Heritage*, Vol. 117, Jan. 1982, pp. 14-17.

Sampson, Robert J. "The Community." *Crime*. eds. James Q. Wilson and Joan Petersilia. San Francisco: ICS Press, 1995, pp. 193-216.

"SBC Approves Family Statement." *The Christian Century*, Vol. 115, June 17-24, 1998, p. 602.

Southern Baptist Convention. *Annual*, 1941.

"Southern Baptists Vote to Boycott Disney." *The Christian Century*, Vol. 114, July 2-9, 1997, pp. 623-624.

Schmitt, Eric. "Nuclear Families Drop Below 25% of Households for First Time." *The New York Times*. 15 May 2001, p. A1.

Schucking, Levin L. *The Puritan Family: A Social Study from the Literary Sources*. New York: Schocken Books, 1969.

Schussler-Fiorenza, Elizabeth. *In Memory of Her*. New York: Crossroads, 1983.

Sennett, Richard. *Families Against the City: Middle-Class Homes of Industrial Chicago*, 1872-1890. Cambridge: Harvard University Press, 1970.

Shahar, Shulamith. *Childhood in the Middle Ages*. London: Routledge, 1990.

Shapiro, Joseph P. "The Faith Factor: Can Churches Cure America's Social Ills?" *U. S. News & World Report*, 9 Sept. 1996, p. 47.

Shipps, Jan. *Mormonism: The Story of a New Religious Tradition.* Urbana: University of Illinois, 1985.

Slater, Peter Gregg. *Children in the New England: In Death and In Life.* Hamden: Archon Books, 1977.

Sontag, Frederick. *Sun Myung Moon and the Unification Church.* Nashville: Abingdon, 1977.

Sommerville, John. *The Rise and Fall of Childhood.* New York: Vintage Books, 1982.

Spaulding, John D. "Bonding in the Bleachers: A Visit to the Promise Keepers." *Christian Century*, 113:8, 6 March, 1996, p. 263.

Stack, Steven. "The Effect of Domestic/Religious Individualism on Suicide, 1954-1978." *Journal of Marriage and Family*, 47, No. 2, May 1985: pp. 431-447.

Stackhouse, Max L. *Covenant and Commitments: Faith, Family, and Economic Life.* Kentucky: Westminster John Knox Press, 1997.

Steiner, Gilbert Y. *The Futility of Family Policy.* Washington, DC: The Brookings Institution, 1981.

Stone, Lawrence. *The Family, Sex and Marriage in England: 1500-1800.* New York: Harper & Row, 1977.

"The Decline of the Two-Parent Family." *U. S. News & World Report*, 19 Feb. 1996, p. 22.

Thomas, Darwin L. and Gwendolyn C. Henry. "The Religion and Family Connection: Increasing Dialogue in the Social Sciences." *Journal of Marriage and Family*, 47, No. 2, May 1985: pp. 369-379.

Thornton, Arland and Donald Camburn. "Religious Participation and Adolescent Sexual Behavioral Attitudes." *Journal of Marriage and Family*, 51, No. 3, Aug. 1989: pp. 641-653.

Thornton, Arland, William G. Axinn and Daniel H. Hill. "Reciprocal Effects of Religiosity, Cohabitation and Marriage." *American Journal of Sociology*, 98, No. 3, 1992: pp. 629-651.

Trattner, Walter I. *Crusade for the Children: A History of the National Child Labor Committee and Child Labor Reform in America.* Chicago: Quadrangle Books, 1970.

Trueheart, Charles. "Welcome to the Next Church." *The Atlantic Monthly*, Aug. 1996.

United States. Department of Commerce. Economics and Statistics Administration. *Statistical Abstract of the United States, 1995.* 115th ed. Bureau of the Census. 1995.

Veyne, Paul. "The Roman Empire." *A History of Private Life.* Vol. 1, eds. Aries and Duby. Cambridge: Belknap Press, 1987, pp. 5-207.

Wadsworth, Benjamin. *The Well-Ordered Family.* Boston, 1712.

Wallerstein, Judith S. and Sandra Blakeslee. *Second Chances: Men, Women, and Children a Decade After Divorce.* New York: Ticknor & Fields, 1989.

Wemple, Suzanne F. *Women in Frankish Society: Marriage and the Cloister.* Philadelphia: University of Pennsylvania, 1981.

Wilkinson, Melvin L. and William C. Tanner III. "The Influence of Family Size, Interaction and Religiosity on Family Affection in a Mormon Sample." *Journal of Marriage and Family*, Vol. 42, 1980: pp. 297-304.

Witte, John Jr. *From Sacrament to Contract: Marriage, Religion, and Law in the Western Tradition.* Kentucky: Westminster John Knox Press, 1997.

Woodward, Kenneth L. "The Gospel of Guyhood." *Newsweek.* 29 August. 1994, pp. 60-61.

World Wide Marriage Encounter [online]. Aug. 2000. Available from World Wide Web: *<http://WWME.org>*.

Wray, Herbert. "A Georgia Farmer Takes Stock." *U. S. News & World Report.* 9 Dec. 1996, p. 86.

Zelizer, Vivianna A. *Pricing the Priceless Child: The Changing Social Value of Children.* New York: Basic Books, 1985.

Zipperer, John. "'True Love Waits' Now Worldwide Effort." *Christianity Today.* Vol. 38, 18 July 1994, p. 58.

Index